The Partnership Marriage

Creating the Life You Love...Together

Andrew L. Miser, Ph.D.

Cover Design by Mark Tatro
Cover Artwork by Amanda Freymann
Author Photograph by Joel DeGrand

ISBN: 149915772X
ISBN 13: **9781499157727**

TABLE OF CONTENTS

DEDICATION

This book is dedicated to Martha,
my best friend, true love, wife and partner for 39 years,
and
to Wendel and Mary,
my twin for 64 years, and his best friend, true love,
wife and partner for 41 years

July 16, 2014

Lauren,

Thank you for your
advice and counsel!

Andy

ACKNOWLEDGMENTS

The first person I wish to acknowledge is my longtime friend Bob Mauterstock. Bob asked me several years ago, after hearing for the umpteenth time that I was interested in writing a book on partnership in marriage, "Hey, Andy, when are you going to write your book?" For the past two years, he has held my feet to the fire and routinely emailed me or called me to ask me how the project was proceeding. He, more than anyone, supported me in bringing my vision to reality.

Wendy Capland, another close friend, has routinely supported and coached me in clarifying my goals and in being fearless in my commitment. She invited me to be a guest on her community television program where I spoke about my commitment to partnership marriage. She has been like a rock in supporting my professional development and in being bold in my choices.

Years ago, at the mid-point of my career as a psychologist, I re-trained as a marriage and family therapist. I wish to thank Les Strong for all the years of teaching and peer support in mastering the art of working with couples and families in therapy. I also want to thank Gijs Surie, who, as a good friend and mentor, championed my development as a professional coach when Martha and I lived in The Netherlands. Later, after four years in Amsterdam and our return to Boston, I worked with Clark Friedrichs, a coach, trainer and coach supervisor at the Coaches Training Institute, who helped me to clarify the focus of my coaching and make the shift from couples therapist to couples coach. Thank you, Clark, for your extraordinary support in my transformation.

I thank Bob Stegman who helped me design my first professional website for my new business enterprise. I also greatly appreciate the tireless work of Kate Hyland Mercer, Kelley Norton and Tim Ludy at Business Concepts, Inc., who expanded and refined my website, helped me learn to blog, publish a newsletter and use social media in productive ways.

Most recently, I have been working with the Chief Penguin, Michael Katz, at Blue Penguin Development, a marketing firm for solo professionals. Michael has helped me alter the way I was thinking about marketing and find my voice in the public arena. When I kept trying to make it complicated, Michael made marketing much simpler. Michael, thank you for that and for introducing me to Belinda Wasser, who has taught me that it is really okay to ask for help when I don't know how to negotiate all the new Internet technologies available today for the independent solo professional. Belinda's business is called Rocket Girl Solutions. Thank you, Rocket Girl!

I particularly want to thank Lauren Hidden who provided me with a manuscript review and many brilliant suggestions as to how to improve the manuscript. The project was effectively stopped until I met and spoke to her. I also want to thank Lauren for editing the manuscript and Jeanne Connell for proofreading the final draft of the book.

I feel most honored to have been able to have Amanda Freymann create the artwork for my book cover. She has been in the publishing business for years and is simply a master at her craft. Amanda painted a beautiful watercolor of the Amish double wedding ring design, which is a pattern often used in making quilts. We both felt that a quilt is a wonderful metaphor for the life couples weave over a lifetime. Thank you, Amanda, for who you have been for me throughout my life both as a sister-in-law and as a friend. Special thanks also goes to Mark Tatro of Rotate Graphics for designing the book cover and to Joel DeGrand whose photograph of me graces the back of the book.

I want to thank all the couples I worked with in my therapy practice, the couples I have coached and the couples who have taken my partnership programs. All of you have expertly trained me in the work I am so passionate about today. Martha and I are blessed to have many friends who enjoy the fruits of a long and happy marriage. Thank you for your abiding friendship and for all the times when we shared and laughed together. You know who you are!

Ruth and Jeff Freymann, my parents-in-law, who have been married for over 63 years, and Jody and Hugh Miser, my parents, who were married two days short of 55 years, provided Martha and me with clear models for lifelong partnership in marriage. Thank you for being constant, shining beacons of light and, day in and day out, exemplars of partnership marriage.

Wendel, I am so happy that you are my twin brother. Thank you for always being there growing up together and for what I have learned about myself and about life itself in relationship with you. Mary, you inspire me with your steadfast and uncompromising love. It shines through in your partnership with Wendel!

I thank my daughter and my son-in-law, Amanda and Josh Reese, my daughter Christina Miser, my son Carl Miser and my three grandsons Broderic, Caiden and Ryland Reese for being my inspiration and for grounding me in why I do the work I do. Having a happy and healthy marriage is great for the couple, but, more importantly, vital for our children and the generations of children who follow. I have always said that the greatest gift you can give your children is having a great marriage.

Martha, when you walked into my life so did a lifetime of joy, wonder and love. Together, we live an extraordinary, magical life. Thank you for sharing your life with me. Thank you for all the dreams we have fulfilled together and for those we have yet to share. Thank you for being my partner in marriage.

MORE RESOURCES FOR YOU!

In addition to the text and examples you'll find within the pages of this book, I have set up a private website for book owners with additional conversational tools, exercises and resources.

Just visit www.thepartnershipmarriagebook.com/tools and use the password "youandme" (no quotes, all lower case) to download these tools to your computer.

Look for the specifics at the end of Chapters 4 through 9.

PROLOGUE

*"When marriage becomes a partnership devoted to worth-
while aims, it gives us more than emotional satisfaction; it
helps to make our lives rich and meaningful."*
                                              —Blaine J. Fowers

I was born in April 1950 an identical twin. My childhood and
my early teenage years orbited around my relationship with
my brother, Wendel. From the moment we were born, we were
defined in relationship with each other. We were "the twins." I was
part of a couple, a twosome, before I became an individual. As
young adults, Wendel and I began to exert our individuality as we
attended separate colleges, got married to extraordinary women,
moved to distinct areas of the country and pursued very different
careers. Before I met Martha in May 1971 and before my life took
off on a whole new orbit, Wendel had been my first real partner
in life.

This book is not about growing up as twins or about being a
twin. It is about creating a fulfilling partnership and an enduring
marriage with your spouse. As I have thought about this subject,
it dawned on me that I learned many lessons about being a good
husband and partner in marriage from my childhood as a twin.
From very early on, I knew that although Wendel and I were alike
in many ways, we were different people, even though our "same-
ness" seemed to be most prominent to everyone else. Although
we were identical twins, we never saw each other as identical. We
saw ourselves as equal. We made sure that we each had the same

opportunities as the other. We took turns. We considered what the other wanted to do. We didn't try to dominate one another or be better than our twin. There were, of course, things that I was better at than Wendel and things that Wendel was better at than I.

Fairness and choice were always important. On our birthday, I might cut the cake and Wendel would choose the first piece. We always made sure that what one of us got, the other got as well. Fairness defined our relationship. We enjoyed being together. I had a ready-made playmate. I had a built-in partner. We were not all that competitive. If we played on the same sports team, we loved to win together. It was much harder when one of us won a sports contest and the other lost. Our yearbook quote was, "United we stand, divided we fall." Equality, fairness, choice and winning together were all important lessons that I learned in my relationship with Wendel. We also learned that we are unique human beings: Each of us has made our own individual contributions in our careers and to people in our lives. Today, we celebrate our individuality as much as we do our twin-ship.

Upon reflection, what my wife, Martha, and I have created in the past 39 years rests on the same set of values. The challenge for me as a twin was to forge my own identity distinct from Wendel's, while ultimately being able to celebrate our twin-ness. My challenge with Martha has been to create a fulfilling and powerful partnership in marriage where we can both express our individuality to the fullest. We learned to view each other's contributions to the health and well-being of our marriage as having an equal value. We learned to care about fairness in our relationship. We learned to honor each other's choices and to consider each other's needs and wants in the choices that we made. We have learned that to have a great life together, our marriage was going to have to work for each of us, individually and collectively, in other words, for "you, me *and* us."

I met Martha at a family picnic on Memorial Day in 1971. My sister, Emily, a freshman in high school, was a close friend of Sarah, one of the daughters in the family who was coming to visit. I had great anticipation about the get-together because Emily had told me that Sarah had an older sister whom they both wanted me to meet. All I knew was that I was going to meet a girl at the afternoon picnic.

I was home in Farmington, Connecticut, from my junior year at Colgate University. That day, I helped Dad get the lawn and pool ready for our visitors, setting up the picnic table and chairs for the festivities. I was standing next to the pool when I saw that our guests had arrived. I then met Dr. and Mrs. John Freymann, and Emily's good friend Sarah. Right behind Sarah a young beautiful woman walked out into the sunlight. My eyes met hers. I could feel her gaze reach into me, something in her touching something in me that communicated simply, "I'm here and I see you." In that moment, I knew something extraordinary was happening. There were no words for it. I (we) just knew.

In our initial conversations, I learned that Martha was headed to Kirkland College in the fall for her freshman year. Kirkland College was only a 25-minute car ride from Colgate in upstate New York. I also learned that she, like me, was a big Red Sox fan. As I got to know her that afternoon, I could feel us stepping into a new friendship. We felt we could be ourselves with each other. Over forty years later, those first special memories of being together that afternoon live for both of us like they happened only yesterday.

Martha and I dated for three years. I graduated from Colgate and completed my Master's degree in developmental psychology at the University of Nebraska while she attended her first three undergraduate years at Kirkland. She visited me in Lincoln, Nebraska, in October of 1972 and I asked her to marry me. My proposal was quite impulsive, and honestly, not well thought out.

I knew I loved her and wanted to spend my life with her. Martha didn't answer right away; in fact, it was not until a year later that she asked *me* to marry *her*. It was then that our life's journey really began.

Today, after raising three children, earning our Ph.D. degrees, building our careers, putting our adult children through college, celebrating the wedding of our eldest daughter and being at the births of our three grandchildren, we are still together, creating a fulfilling life. Getting married to each other was *the* most important choice we have made in our lives. Looking back, when we made that choice, we honestly had no clue what it was going to take to be successful, happy and fulfilled in our marriage over a lifetime. The one thing we did know was that we wanted to be with each other. We loved each other and we wanted to make the commitment that would allow us to be together for the rest of our lives: Get married. We had no clue how it would all turn out.

At that time, our understanding of marriage was rooted in our experiences growing up in families of the 1950s. Our fathers had careers and were the primary breadwinners of the family, and our mothers were the primary caregivers who raised our siblings and us and took care of the household responsibilities. Today, this model of marriage is referred to as the traditional model of marriage. By the early 1970s, social attitudes around sexual activity were changing quickly, and many people were choosing to live together prior to getting married. Studying at Kirkland College, a new and liberal arts college for women, Martha was very familiar with much of the feminist literature and was well aware of the legal and social pressures that were at work to improve the rights of women in the United States.

When we got married in August 1974, we had a personal commitment to each other, a model for the way marriage was supposed to be and an awareness of great social upheaval that was underway in the country. In hindsight, we were unprepared for how much we were both going to be required to change over the next four decades to have our marriage work. We had heard that being married was going to take a lot of work and commitment, but we really had no idea what that meant. Like many couples, we had few real skills. We learned how to be married like most young adults: By the seat of our pants. All we knew was that we wanted to be together. Beyond that, we really didn't know what it was we wanted for our lives or how we would figure that out. We also had no idea how the institution of marriage in the United States was going to change over the next 40 years.

The statistics on marriage over the last three decades of the twentieth century have revealed that many thousands of married couples have failed at creating fulfilling marriages. The statistics suggested that the chances of having a successful, long-term marriage were the same as flipping a coin: one in every two. Even then, if you were one of those couples whose marriage did last a lifetime, the possibility of having a fulfilling partnership in your marriage was not guaranteed.

In the first decade of the twenty-first century, the divorce rate appears to be declining. Less than 50% of individuals, however, are now choosing marriage, compared to 80% of individuals 50 years ago. Many people are also choosing to marry at a later age and are adopting other kinds of lifestyles, such as single parenthood and cohabitation. Also, by the end of the second decade of this century, it is likely that *all* people will have the opportunity to legally marry the person they love, regardless of their sexual orientation.

For twenty-five years, I trained and practiced as a psychologist and a marriage and family therapist in Hartford, Connecticut. My greatest joy was working with young couples raising children with developmental and medical disabilities. The heartache these couples often experienced was crushing and, yet their commitment to and unconditional love for their children were inspiring. They worked hard at staying in communication and being a team as they dealt with unrelenting and very difficult circumstances. I learned a lot about resilience and the transformative power of creating positive meaning to restore a sense of family cohesion and well-being when confronted by life's difficult dilemmas (Patterson, 1991; Miser & Rosano, 2006).

In 2002, Martha accepted an expatriate position at an international bank in The Netherlands and we moved our family to Amsterdam. In Europe, I re-trained as a professional coach with the Coaches Training Institute. I focused my coaching work on helping American expatriate couples adjust to life as global citizens and deal effectively with all the challenges inherent in moving to a foreign country (Miser & Miser, 2009). Couples who take on such an extraordinary commitment discover very quickly that, to be successful in living internationally, there is one imperative to which they must pay attention: Partnership. As a result of this work, I became interested in educating and coaching couples in how to strengthen their connection with each other and to sustain an enthusiasm for their marriage over the long term. I was curious about providing married couples with tools that would empower them to fulfill their aspirations and their dreams together. What tools can couples use that will allow them to create a lifelong partnership that is active, enduring and full of vigor each and every day? What conversations enable couples to design a life they love... together?

I admire people who take on big challenges. Astronauts who launch into space and people who climb to the top of Mount Everest amaze me with their courage. I cheer and marvel at the commitment of Olympic athletes, scientists who discover cures for devastating diseases and novelists who write books that make the bestseller list. I am truly inspired, though, by couples who marry and live a lifetime together, supporting each other in fulfilling their dreams. My parents were married well over fifty years. My parents-in-law have been married over sixty years. While their marriages began at an earlier time and may have looked different from the marriages of today, theirs have been no less a partnership.

I hold marriage as an extraordinary opportunity to grow together and to develop a mature partnership in life. While love is necessary, it does not seem sufficient in building an enduring, fulfilling life together. Over time, I have become intrigued with the idea that the quality of marriage is enhanced through the kinds of conversations that you, as a couple, have with each other. You create partnership in your marriage through the values you hold dear, through the vision of the life you share and through the thousands of conversations you have together.

The Focus of this Book

The focus of this book is the power of conversation in marriage and how you and your partner, by having important conversations, can create a life you love. You'll learn what it will take for you to create a mature partnership in your marriage, one that lasts a lifetime.

As you read, ask yourself these questions: What do my spouse and I want in our life together? What is really important to us in our marriage? What are our deepest desires? What dreams have we been putting off for years? What is possible for us? What are we passionate about? What is holding us back? What is the quality of our partnership? How can we better work together to create the life we desire? As you read this book, I invite you to have conversations with your spouse for expanding and enriching the quality of your marriage.

Several caveats are necessary. In this book I explore how marriage has developed in the United States and Western Europe. For instance, I talk about the societal changes that have taken place in the past sixty years and how the public discourse in American society has transformed the institution of marriage itself. I do not, however, examine marriage in other cultures, although what I am offering may have applicability to people from other countries. Also, I acknowledge I am a heterosexual white male who grew up in upper middle class privilege in New England. I offer this only to reveal potential bias that may be inherent in the way in which I am viewing marriage. My own lived experience clearly excludes a rich array of experiences of people from different socioeconomic, ethnic and sexual orientation groups and from different geographical regions of the country. And since I am male, I acknowledge that, while I have worked very hard at it for over forty years, I still fall short in being able to see the world from a woman's point of view. You can ask my wife, Martha, about that. I am very aware that to understand the changes that marriage has undergone in the last six decades, you need to understand how the legal rights and opportunities for women changed in the United States during that time.

My intention is not to give you a lot of advice about how you should express partnership in your lives. Every partnership marriage is distinct. Partnership, ultimately, is a context for marriage and how you create partnership in your marriage is through the commitments you make and the conversations you have. You won't be learning strategies on how to deal with specific issues around money, sex, spirituality, illness, infidelity, etc. Many of these issues are best dealt with in marital therapy or with professionals who have specific expertise.

This book is designed to both give you a framework to think of your marriage as a long-term partnership and provide different tools in the form of conversations that you can use to design your life together. This book is not about fixing your marriage; it is about creating the life that you desire. Toward this end, I have brought together ideas from many different fields of study, including life span development, marriage education, leadership development and professional coaching. Your marriage and your partnership are the vehicles for you to live lives you both love and to love the life you share. If you are committed to having an enduring, fulfilling partnership as well as a happy and healthy lifelong marriage, this book is for you.

A Walk in Vondelpark

Martha and I strolled along in Vondelpark on a beautiful late summer day, as we were apt to do just before dinnertime when we were living in Amsterdam in 2005. The air that day was clear, the clouds lay suspended against the bluish-grey sky and the leaves in the trees danced in the breeze. People rode by on their bicycles in all directions: some very leisurely and some at a fast clip. Parents walked with their children in baby carriages and at their side, as did pet owners with their dogs. Skateboarders and joggers flew by and groups of teenagers milled about with no clear purpose other than hanging out together in the park. Jugglers and musicians held the attention of onlookers, families picnicked together on the spacious green lawn and lovers on blankets rimmed the glimmering pond at the center of the park. We walked together, taking in the smorgasbord of sights, sounds and sensations in Vondelpark, which was located near where we lived in the southeastern part of the city. We loved this routine.

I felt deeply connected with Martha on this walk. Although we were in a new and foreign city, away from family and friends in the United States, I felt peaceful, grounded and at home. It had not always been like that, particularly in recent years. After living for twenty-five years in Hartford, Connecticut, Martha and I had uprooted our family at the mid-point of our careers to move to Amsterdam, where Martha took an expatriate position at a well-known Dutch bank, and I took a hiatus from a career as a psychologist and marriage and family therapist. I became a "house husband," taking care of the home and our growing children, all of whom experienced difficult adjustments as a result of our move.

There were many times Martha and I felt disconnected and dislocated and wondered, "What were we thinking?"

As we walked along, I felt an urge to have a conversation with Martha to explore what had allowed us to be so bold and adventurous to have made the choice to move to Amsterdam. I asked her if she'd have a conversation with me about our relationship at this stage of our lives. She was more than glad to engage with me.

I asked her, "When we are in touch with our relationship and with what we have together, what is present in our lives?" Without hesitation, she said to me, "A sense that anything is possible." Her response resonated with me. I could see that when we are together and aware of our commitment to the quality of marriage, we have a feeling that we can be or do anything. Life is wonderful. Life is grand. I reflected that when we first met, when we had each of our three children, when we supported each other in getting our advanced degrees and when we moved to The Netherlands, we had *that* sense that, "anything is possible."

Now I was even more curious. I asked her again, "When we are in touch with our relationship, what do we experience together?" This time she paused in thought as we continued down the path. In that moment, we took in the surroundings and all of the activity around us. She said, "Being excited about the life we are creating." I flashed back on the early days of our marriage, when we were first dating and how excited we were about being with each other. I could hear the narrative over our life's journey that had allowed us to continuously return to being enthusiastic about our relationship. The story line had not always been happy or joyous, far from it, but we had worked together over the years to consistently experience that familiar place we call "us," where we have been able to be enthusiastic about our lives and passionate about what we have shared together.

We kept exploring this notion of "us," that space only the two of us have known, have nurtured and have honored for so long.

I then said, "There is partnership." When I sat on the plane next to Martha as we flew to Amsterdam for the first time three years previously, I thought, "I am sitting next to my partner in life. I wouldn't do this with anyone else." When Martha and I are most deeply in touch with our relationship, we know that anything is possible, we are passionate about our life together and we are full partners. We can tackle anything.

As we continued this generative, creative dialogue in the park, I started to wonder what had given us the ability to have this quality of relationship. I posed another question for us to consider, "What has allowed us to reliably create and share the experience of possibility, passion and partnership?" As we strolled along, we were oblivious to all that was going on around us. The park and all its activity had seemingly disappeared. All that was happening was the conversation in which we were engaged.

"Commitment," she said. "We have been able to sustain our commitment to the quality of our relationship and our lives." Commitment over the years has been an essential ingredient in our marriage. Without commitment, renewed and matured over time, we would not have had a relationship that endured, we likely would not have had the quality of experience we have shared and we certainly would not have been willing to take the risks we had taken over the years. We have routinely and regularly recommitted to the commitment we made almost four decades ago.

We considered the question again, "What has allowed us to create a relationship where we have been able to reliably share an experience of possibility, passion and partnership?" This time, I blurted, "Alignment." Martha and I have not always agreed on everything. In fact, we couldn't imagine having such a relationship. What we have shared has been the ability to have conversations about what is important to each of us and to be in alignment about what we care about. Over the years, we have been aligned in our values, in what is going to work for our relationship, in our vision of our future and in the quality of life we are committed to. Like commitment, alignment has been an important framework for our relationship.

We were now on a roll. I noticed how engaged we were in this conversation. As we considered the question we had before us once more, Martha said, "Understanding." Martha and I have taken great care to listen and to hear each other over the years. Often, it has been effortless; at other times, it has taken a great deal of work. What has been important, though, is that we have been committed to understanding each other. Like commitment and alignment, understanding each other has been another essential ingredient that has allowed us to have a marriage that is both satisfying and always growing.

We considered the question one last time, "What has allowed us to create a relationship where we have been able to share an experience of possibility, passion and partnership?" First, Martha said, "Play," then, I said, "Appreciation." While our marriage had been a long and winding road to that point, Martha and I have learned how to play. As I reflected on our life together, I was reminded of the laughter and the fun we have shared. We have reliably made sure that, no matter how hard we work, we have room in our relationship for play. We have also appreciated each other and our relationship. Issues, difficulties and arguments have, at times, dampened our spirits and caused us to disconnect from each other. Yet, we have been able to sustain and continually recreate that sense of gratitude for what we contribute to each other and what we have in our lives. Being thankful and appreciative of our relationship has allowed us to continually see the quality and richness of our lives.

In our brief stroll around Vondelpark that day, Martha and I tapped into the wisdom of our relationship. For forty-five minutes on a Saturday afternoon in August in a foreign land, we had simply had a conversation; just the two of us. In our marriage, we have been committed to each other, been aligned in what matters most, taken care to understand each other, been playful together and been appreciative of each other and our relationship. These have been essential ingredients for our life together.

Since that day in the park with Martha, I have wondered about what other couples share in their lives together, the quality of other marriages and what I could contribute. I have wondered about the difference I could make in teaching and coaching couples in how to create and share a fulfilling marriage over a lifetime. I have been intrigued how marriage has changed over the past sixty years and how different it has been for Martha and me from our parents' marriages of the 1950s and 60s. I have wondered about why the divorce rate had skyrocketed in the last three decades of the twentieth century. I have also thought about what it is going to take to give couples the tools and the skills to consistently and reliably fulfill their dreams inside of their marriages. How can I support couples to stay committed through thick and thin, through sickness and in health and until "death do us part"? My passion for my own marriage and curiosity about the long-term health and vibrancy of the institution of marriage brought me to writing this book and to giving couples who are committed to lifelong partnership conversational tools to create the life they love...together.

Chapter

1

THE DAWNING OF A
NEW DAY FOR MARRIAGE

*"Today, we are entering uncharted territory, and there is
still no definitive guide to the new marital landscape."*
                                                    –Stephanie Coontz

A Recent History of Marriage

My parents were married in 1944 just as the war was ending
in Europe. Martha's parents married six years later in 1950. Both
of our sets of parents were exemplars of a particular model of
marriage that had been evolving for over two hundred years and
had become widely adopted across North America and Western
Europe. At that time there was little questioning that, in marriage,
the husband's job was to work outside the home and earn the family's income and the wife's job was to care for the children and
manage the household (Coontz, 2005). There was a clear, socially
acceptable division of labor between married men and women.
More importantly, every couple who fell in love had a clear pathway
to a future of fulfillment and happiness: Get married, have children and live happily ever after. This *was* just way it was supposed
to be. On my elementary school playground as a young child, I can
remember reciting a common childhood nursery rhyme of the

era that captured this universal phenomenon: "First comes love, then comes marriage, then comes baby in the baby carriage." The golden age of traditional male breadwinner and female home-maker marriage had reached its zenith (Coontz, 2005).

At the time my our parents were getting married, a Lutheran pastor and a well-known speaker on practical family matters, Dr. O.A. Geiseman, published a small book on marriage called *Make Yours a Happy Marriage*. In the book, Dr. Geiseman gave advice to wives on obeying their husbands:

> Where the relationship is right and where the husband is considerate of his wife and the wife is appreciative of her husband's love, there most decisions will be reached by mutual agreement, so that marriage becomes what is commonly termed a fifty-fifty proposition. Despite all this, however, it still remains a fact that final decisions and final directions should rest with the husband. A woman who can-not and does not regard her husband as the head of the house is not to be envied but pitied, for no woman under such circumstances will ever truly be happy (p. 19).

When giving advice to husbands, Dr. Geiseman wrote that people:

> ...who view marriage purely in the light of reason and human experience confirm...that for an ideal marriage the husband should earn the living while the wife devotes herself to the duties of home. No doubt many homes would have been saved had this rule been observed (p. 11).

During the 1950s, 80% of all young adults adopted this male breadwinner and female homemaker model of marriage as the primary path they could take toward adulthood (Coontz, 2005).

Couples began marrying younger and divorce rates fell after the war. With improvements in the American economy that resulted in a dramatic increase in the standard of living and a doubling of disposable income, most married couples could begin to fulfill the "American Dream" of owning their own private home and raising a family. Men focused on their careers and economic success, while women stayed home raising their children and learning to use all the household appliances and conveniences that were being manufactured in the post-war American economy (Coontz, 2005). In the American family of the 1950s, husbands and wives turned inward toward hearth and home. Their central focus was on participating in their nuclear family and expressing shared values of comfort, togetherness and family happiness.

Twenty years later, couples like Martha and me, who were married in the 1970s, had grown up inside this breadwinner/homemaker view of marriage as "the way it should be." At the same time, though, in their teenage and formative years, young people were becoming aware of many legal and social inequities in the wider society that would have a significant impact on their future view of marriage. During the 1960s and early 1970s, the civil rights movement, peace protests over the Vietnam War and the women's rights movement swept the United States. The latter movement, particularly, challenged the existing marital roles between men and women and even called into question the whole institution of marriage itself. In the beginning of 1960, 60% of all marriages had adopted the male breadwinner/female homemaker model of marriage. By 1985, only 10% of marriages represented this kind of arrangement (Collins, 2009). It took generations to establish the "traditional model" of marriage and only a few years for it to come to an end (Coontz, 2005).

The establishment of laws that prohibited discrimination on the basis of sex in the workplace, medical advances in birth control and the passage of Roe v. Wade in 1973 all gave women authority over their own bodies, the choice to have children or not and new opportunities in the workplace. Many mothers of the 1950s saw a new future for their daughters and encouraged them as they grew into young women in the 1970s to move away from the role of housewife, to go to college and to start their own careers (Coontz, 2005). Women increasingly put off getting married and having children until later.

Marriage in the 1970s, at the time when Martha and I were embarking on our own marital journey, was being redefined as a *legal* entity between two *equal* partners (Coontz, 2005). Legal precedents of this period forced a societal re-examination of the roles of men and women in marriage. "Head and master" laws, which determined the legal relationship between a husband and his wife in marriage, had been in existence since the time when the early colonialists had arrived from England. These laws were based on the doctrine of "coverture," which held that a couple became one person when they got married and that one person legally was the husband (Cherlin, 2011). By the mid-1970s, such laws that had given husbands the authority to have the final say with respect to all household and jointly held property without his wife's knowledge or consent were being challenged and abolished in all fifty states. It was not until 1975 that a woman could freely get a mortgage or a credit card without her husband's co-signature. The legal structures that gave married men the power to unilaterally make financial and legal decisions were collapsing. This ushered in an extraordinary new opportunity for married couples to participate as *equal* human beings in their marriages under their own roofs.

During this time of re-examination, young men and women began casting off the time-honored rituals of marriage. Couples wrote their own vows and established their own marriage contracts in an attempt to honor and value true equality in their relationship. New alternative pathways to adulthood were on the rise for individuals and couples, such as unwed cohabitation, out-of-wedlock childrearing and single lifestyles. Many young adults of the 1970s wrestled with their parents over issues of living together and having sex prior to marriage. Getting married was clearly now a personal choice, one option among many for most young people and, if a couple did choose to get married, there were many forms of experimentation and self-expression that marriages could take.

In 1974, the year Martha and I got married, I completed my Master's degree while Martha finished her junior year at Kirkland. She went home to live with her parents that summer to help her mother and father prepare for the wedding that was scheduled for August. Martha was adamant that our wedding not be held in a church, so she and her parents settled on the backyard of their beautiful Farmington home that could easily accommodate 120 people. Martha did not want to wear a fancy or expensive wedding dress, so she and her mother went out and bought a simple off-white peasant dress. With Martha's help, I bought a green plaid polyester jacket with white pants, a green bow tie and platform shoes! To this day, Martha and I both smile when we look at our wedding portrait and say, "What were we thinking?"

Martha didn't want a typical wedding cake either. She ended up ordering a four-layer, square, chocolate cake in which each layer was kitty-corner to the layer of cake below it. Martha didn't want her wedding to be catered. As a result, her mother made enough chicken tetrazzini for the entire gathering. Lastly, Martha and I wanted to write our own marriage vows. In the vows that we took, we each declared that we would be together "for as long as we both shall *love*," not live. Quite coincidently, we were married on the day after President Richard Nixon resigned from the oval office and on the day the *New York Times* declared: "The Nightmare is Over."

Our marriage on August 10, 1974 reflected some of the values of the 1970s while honoring the traditional values of our parents' generation. That day, we had a sense that one era was ending while another was just beginning as the new president, Gerald Ford, was stepping into the White House. Looking back, our marriage was a prototype of many of the marriages that were happening all across America. Martha and I had rebelled against the social and sexual mores of our parents' generation: We had lived together for four months in Lincoln, Nebraska while Martha was a visiting student at the university there, we had an active sexual life prior to getting married and we had challenged the conventions around our wedding. A week after our wedding, when we moved to Clinton, New York to live together during Martha's senior year at Kirkland, she may have been the only married student in her senior class. Kirkland College was a very liberal women's college at the time. The fact that Martha and I had gotten married prior to her graduating from college, and that most all of our friends were progressive young women, many of whom were lesbian, was practically antithetical to what our parents' generation had experienced. Martha and I felt that we were breaking all the rules!

Because many of the traditional rules around getting married were being cast aside, we no longer had a clear rulebook for how to proceed in having our marriage work. We wanted to have a marriage based in equality, fairness and choice; we just didn't know how to go about creating that. My father had always taken care of the finances. So, *obviously*, it was my job to manage the budget and pay the bills, that is, until the day that Martha walked into our shared study six months after we were married and asked me if she could take over managing our finances. I was completed flustered and upset by that simple request. THAT was the man's job; it was my responsibility. I capitulated and gave up that job to her, while holding on to resentment for several years. In those first years of marriage, we hadn't quite figured out who was going to do what around the house. Many chores went unattended to as we went about a very haphazard way of getting our daily household tasks done. Our default way of operating was to do things together, like shopping or doing the laundry at the Laundromat. Life in the early days of our marriage was not all that complicated, so this worked most of the time.

In the first three years of our marriage, Martha completed her college education, worked at a local travel agency and then earned her Master's degree at the Maxwell School of Public Administration at Syracuse University. During this same time, I worked as a developmental therapist at a local preschool program for children with developmental disabilities. We were very much on the track that we would both work and have careers. That was the new model of life for many couples. The neatly delineated marital roles of the 1950s and early 1960s were a thing of the past. While we thought of ourselves as choosing this lifestyle of two careers because of the new opportunities for women to go to college and enter the workforce, we were not as aware that this was also a lifestyle that was in many ways being thrust upon us as a result of the recession and inflation of the 1970s. We both *had* to work to have our marriage work! The average cost of a new home in the 1970s and early 80s had tripled due to the fact that so many baby boomers were now competing in the real estate market (Collins, 2009). It was the first time since the end of World War II that Americans experienced a decline in real income and in purchasing power (Coontz, 2005). That economic decline would last for the next two decades and beyond.

In the first twenty years of our relationship, from 1971 to 1990, everything changed (Collins, 2009). Coontz (2005) wrote:

The whole legal, political and economic context for marriage was transformed. By the end of the 1970s women had access to legal rights, education, birth control, and decent jobs. Suddenly divorce was easy to get. At the same time, traditional family arrangements became more difficult to sustain in the new economy. And new sexual mores, growing tolerance for out-of-wedlock births, and rising aspirations for self-fulfillment changed the cultural milieu in which people made decisions about their personal relation- ships. During the 1980s and 1990s, all these changes came together to irrevocably transform the role of marriage in society at large and in peoples' personal lives (pp. 260-261).

By the end of the twentieth century, American family life looked very different than that of the 1950s. At this time, 62% of all couples had two careers and were dealing with a whole new set of issues as a result of earning dual incomes (Coontz, 2005). Both careers and incomes were now critical to the financial success of the family. In 1978, Martha and I moved to Hartford, Connecticut, returning to where we had met and to be closer to our families. I began doc- toral work in psychology at the University of Connecticut, while Martha got a job as a budget analyst for the City of Hartford. After two years, I took a job with the State of Connecticut at one of the two state institutions for the developmentally disabled. I did this for two reasons: I was figuring out what I wanted to do profession- ally, and we needed two incomes if we were going to afford buying a home. In the fall of 1980, that is exactly what we did. We pur- chased our first home in a southwest neighborhood of Hartford.

By that time, Martha and I had to become much more effec- tive at negotiating all the responsibilities that came with owning a home and, later, with raising children. By the time we started having children in 1984, we felt an imperative that both of us, as partners, be involved in parenting. This was an exciting time, but also a confusing time. As a new father, I had not had a model of fatherhood that included sharing household tasks and parenting. Like me, many men during this time took up the challenge of being more involved in sharing housework; many others did not. In fact, most married women continued to carry the lion's share of childcare and household responsibilities, in addition to working full time.

The legal, economic and social changes in the 1970s and 1980s put enormous pressure on married couples to work together in almost every sphere of their relationship: parenting, managing the finances, taking care of the home, balancing work and home life, nurturing their relationship and keeping in touch with friends and family. Since there was no clear societal script, as there had been in the 1950s, it seemed that *everything* in our life had to be considered and talked about. We, like so many other couples, had to learn to have all kinds of new conversations for negotiating, problem solving, planning, resolving conflicts, envisioning the future and completing projects. I remember that while I was training to be a psychologist, I'd go into a bookstore and find that the self-help section had expanded to include numerous self-improvement books devoted to helping individuals and couples manage their lives and their relationships successfully.

In the last thirty years of the twentieth century, both men and women experienced much higher levels of stress as a result of having to balance their commitments at home and at work. During this time, one in every two American couples was ending their marriages. The odds of getting a divorce were the same as getting heads or tails when flipping a coin! This startling statistic didn't match people's aspirations. The dream of getting married to a loving spouse remained as strong as ever for most young adults. In one recent survey, 90% of individuals still said that getting married was a lifelong dream (Harrar & DeMaria, 2000). Many couples who entered marriage with the idea that marriage would make them happy and fulfill them, however, found themselves lacking many practical relationship skills for making their marriage work over the long haul. For many individuals, what was required for a long-term commitment to marriage was well beyond their skill set.

At the turn of the millennium, Fowers (2000) suggested that both love and emotional gratification that comes from making the commitment to marry were no longer *enough* to have a marriage work. He wrote that the best marriages are "partnerships in which spouses are devoted to creating a shared life," rather than being focused on emotional gratification in their marriage. It isn't any longer about what you individually are going to get out of your marriage; it is what you both are going to put into your marriage that is going to make the difference. It was and still is important that married couples be able to sustain their love for each other over a lifetime. If couples are truly committed to having a fulfilling and loving life together over forty or fifty years, what may be even more important is their ability to create enduring partnership in their marriage.

Marriage Today

Entering the second decade of the twenty-first century, just over half of the adults in the United States were getting married, according to the Pew Research Center (Cohn, et. al., 2011). It was also predicted that the marital rate might drop below 50% in the next few years. Compared to previous generations of Americans, fewer and fewer people are tying the knot. Unlike women sixty years ago, women today have greater economic power, more social independence and higher educational status, all of which have impacted lower marriage rates (Cherlin, 2009). What is interesting, as well, is that the divorce rate is also declining. Although fewer adults are getting married today, those couples who are may have learned better relationship skills to be successful in marriage than in previous decades. Also, quite possibly more and more people are being honest and realistic not only about what it takes to get married, but also about what is required to stay married over a lifetime.

Couples who do marry are generally putting off marriage until later. They are choosing instead to cohabitate, live together with their single friends, or stay at home with their parents. Some women and men are choosing single parenthood over marriage.

Compared to the 1950s when young adults viewed marriage as *the* main pathway to adulthood, many people today see marriage as one path among many to a fulfilling and happy life. For couples that choose this pathway, marriage is viewed as an expression of their commitment to grow as individuals and develop a partnership with their spouse in creating a life of shared values and meaning.

Marriage today has become a "capstone" for many young adults (Cherlin, 2009). Rather than being the foundation of adult life, it is the culmination of a number of accomplishments or milestones that mark the reaching of adulthood for a couple. It is a choice that many couples are making *after* they have completed their education, have lived together for a time and have started their careers.

Research today suggests that married couples are happier, are healthier, have longer lives, are wealthier and have better sex lives than couples who divorce or individuals who remain single (Waite & Gallagher, 2000). Yet, these positive benefits of marriage, the deleterious impact of divorce on children and the hotly contested debates over same-sex marriage have plunged the United Stages into the midst of marriage wars (Cherlin, 2009). Many people support a return to the traditional model of heterosexual marriage in an attempt to recreate that of an earlier time. Many other people, including myself, argue that, since marriage has been completely redefined by law as a union between two equal persons, the right to marry should be extended legally to all citizens, including lesbian and gay people. This group views the choice for gay and lesbian individuals to marry as one of the last true civil rights' battles yet to be waged. As of this writing, it is legal in nineteen states and in the District of Columbia for gay and lesbian individuals to get married, and this issue is being contested in state legislatures across the land.

Today Americans are polarized. While many support same-sex marriage, many others are afraid of the continued decline of the traditional model of marriage between a man and a woman. This polarization fueled an increase in governmental spending for marriage education in the first decade of the twenty-first century. Federal funding for marital education between 2000 and 2010 skyrocketed. In 2006, the United States Congress passed a law providing $150 million per year for marital education projects and research to foster healthy marriage. During this time, marital support and advice exploded on the Internet, nation-wide conferences of marriage educators and experts convened annually, educational programs and workshops for couples increased dramatically and marital coaching gained a solid foothold in the marketplace.

People who have gone to college have an economic advantage over people who only have a high school diploma and who are poor. New evidence shows that those who are most successful at marriage are college educated couples who have the resources to be able to complete their education, start successful careers and plan a family. In contrast, couples with high school diplomas from lower socioeconomic groups fail more frequently at marriage (Cherlin, 2009). Many lower income high school graduates are not marrying, but instead are choosing to live together, putting off marriage indefinitely.

Cherlin (2009) debunks the myth, however, that the poor don't care about having to wait to get married or about finding a person with whom they can share a happy and fulfilling life. He says that just like middle-class and college educated people, high school educated poor people want the *same* thing in life. They want companionship and partnership and to grow and develop throughout their marriage together.

Collins (2009) writes that although women over the last sixty years have accomplished extraordinary things, they still have not yet figured out how to reliably have a fulfilling marriage or a lasting one. To their credit, women have led the way in changing men's attitudes toward the concept of equality for both sexes. Many men today recognize that it isn't just the women's job to "figure out" how to have a lasting, fulfilling marriage. In this time of uncertainty over the future of marriage in our society, all kinds of questions are swirling around. What does a fulfilling, enduring marriage even look like? Is such a marriage possible? Should marriage only be between a man and a woman? Can both individuals in a marriage be happy and fulfilled? Is the institution of marriage really in a state of decline or in a state of metamorphosis or transformation?

One idea seems certain: There is no longer one conception of marriage. There is not one view of who has the right to get married, who goes to work, who takes care of the children, or who handles the household chores. Marriage is whatever a couple makes of it. There is no clear rulebook. Each couple who chooses to get married today creates *their* marriage consistent with their values, their vision, their dreams and their partnership. This new day for marriage is both incredibly challenging on the one hand and extraordinarily exciting on the other.

The Dawning of a New Day for Marriage

In only sixty years, marriage has undergone a dramatic transformation. Despite this, one thing remains unchanged: Getting married and sharing life with a loving partner remains one of the most important and compelling dreams for young people (Harrar & DeMaria, 2007). In a recent survey questioning 1,001 people about their attitudes and beliefs about marriage, the vast majority of the respondents said that having a happy, healthy marriage is an important personal goal for them. 85% of those surveyed said that marriage is fundamentally a partnership between two people and 79% said that the commitment of marriage is lifelong (Harrar and DeMaria, 2007).

Men and women as well as gay and lesbian couples who *can* get married are looking to create a marriage that is mutually satisfying and that allows each partner to not only fulfill their own personal and professional goals, but also the goals of their partnership. Toward this end, everything in marriage must now be negotiated. Society's institutions, laws and customs largely determined the inflexible roles and responsibilities of the 1950s; today's roles and responsibilities are being re-thought and determined by the couples themselves (Coontz, 2005). Coontz (2005) writes that married couples "need to be more intentional about their lives and about the reasons and the rituals that help them stay together." In short, couples today must be equal partners in having their marriage work.

Couples want *the choice and the responsibility* to design their lives together. In today's marriage, it is important for both spouses to have choice over their careers, their lifestyle, their family aspirations and their future. They don't want the roles and responsibilities in their marriage to be dictated by societal institutions. Many women, like men, want to be free to pursue a career. Many men, like women, want to participate in raising their children and taking care of the household routines. Both individuals in the marriage also want to know that they are equal contributors in their marriage and they have fairness in their roles and responsibilities. Building and sustaining a successful marriage requires couples to be able to communicate effectively with each other and to have many more conversations than were required in earlier times. This requires couples to be able to negotiate and talk about *anything and everything* that impacts the quality of their marriage.

Fowers (2000) writes that the best marriages are partnerships in which couples are committed to a life of shared meaning by being in alignment around a set of virtues and values and by having a vision for how those principles are expressed in their lives. He suggests that marriage can be thought of as a partnership that allows couples to be powerfully connected through a shared purpose. He recommends that couples articulate their shared values, design a common vision for their lives and shift their focus from emotional gratification to the quality of their marriage *and* their partnership. He suggests this is a radical view of marriage.

This view of marriage is indeed radical in that couples who consider themselves partners in creating their life together anchor themselves to what is important for each of them individually and for their relationship. They want their marriage to support both partners in fulfilling their dreams and their aspirations. It is *this* commitment to an enduring, fulfilling partnership over a lifetime that is the dawning of a new day for marriage. Partnership marriage is founded in love, choice and equality. It is built through fairness and flexibility, where both spouses grow and develop across their entire life span. Partnership marriage is nurtured through mutual empowerment and, ultimately, shifts the couple's focus to the quality their marital relationship.

The question becomes, how do you co-create a partnership in your marriage? How can your partnership grow and develop over a lifetime? If both of you are developing across a lifelong marriage, marriage must be seen as malleable, changeable, evolving and creative. With the dissolution of defined roles and responsibilities, couples today must be skilled at having conversations about everything in order to have their marriage work. Partnership marriage requires us to see marriage as an inherently creative relationship that is continuously evolving through an emerging network of conversations. The next two chapters will make the case for marriage as a lifelong network of conversations *for* partnership. The nature of these conversations in your marriage will have a great impact in determining the quality and the durability of your marriage and, ultimately, whether your marriage is indeed a partnership or not.

Chapter

2

MARRIAGE AS A CONVERSATION FOR AN ENDURING, FULFILLING PARTNERSHIP

"When entering into a marriage one ought to ask oneself: Do you believe you are going to enjoy talking with this woman up into your old age? Everything else in marriage is transitory, but most of the time you are together will be devoted to conversation."

–Friedrich Nietzsche

Marriage as a Lifelong Conversation

You and every other couple who gets engaged do so with the hope of having a happy marriage that is alive and vigorous over many years. I have never met a couple who on their wedding day intended for their relationship to become unhappy or disintegrate at some point in the future. This is also rarely the hope of the couple's family and friends who witness their exchange of vows on their wedding day. It is safe to say that when most couples enter into marriage, they do so for the purpose of being partners over a lifetime. For partnership to flourish, it is important for you to learn to have meaningful conversations with each other.

In the beginning of a relationship, you and your new friend have conversations to get to know one another. You share aspects of your lives with each other. You exchange ideas, share your feelings and talk about what's important to each of you and, in the process, create your relationship. As your relationship grows and matures, you may begin to talk about what you want for your relationship. Such possibilities might be to have an exclusive, monogamous relationship, to live together or to get married sometime in the future. All along the way, you create your relationship inside of conversations with each other. The nature of these conversations determines the quality of your relationship and, later, if you choose to get married, the health of your marriage. Ultimately, your ability to have effective and productive conversations with each other will determine your experience of partnership, your passion for your marriage and whether your marriage will be enduring.

There are two things I remember most about being with Martha that afternoon in May 1971. First was the moment I met her. I had the experience of being "seen" by her. Martha reported to me later that she had a similar experience. The other thing that I remember most about that day was that we couldn't stop talking with each other. The more we talked, the more I wanted to talk with her. I remember that the entire time I spent with Martha, we were in a conversation. To be truthful, the conversations that we had that day were pretty juvenile and silly. We let each other know, "I like being with you. I'm enjoying talking with you."

We got to know each other simply by starting a conversation that has now been going on for over four decades. Today, we are able to talk about all kinds of things. We've had thousands and thousands of conversations over the years. We've had conversations for play and connecting like we did the first day we met. We've had conversations for understanding each other and our feelings. We've resolved problems and conflicts, negotiated agreements, made all kinds of plans from parties to vacations and designed and carried out numerous home and family projects over the years. These activities and many more have all been accomplished by being able to converse with each other. Our ability to have interesting, rich and meaningful conversations with each other has played a significant role in determining the quality of our marriage and life together.

On the day that Martha and I met, there were also cultural and societal conversations that were shaping Americans' ideas about modern martial relationships. These collective, societal conversations were often out of our awareness, but, nonetheless, impacting the way we thought about our relationship and how we eventually thought about our marriage. Let's take a look at some of the societal conversations that have been shaping marriage for generations.

Societal Conversations that Have Shaped Marriage

For thousands of years prior to the eighteenth century in Europe and elsewhere around the globe, marriage between a man and a woman had little to do with love. Marriage was not about having a lifetime companion and was not even fundamentally about raising children. Marriage was an institution that organized the division of labor between men and women and legitimized economic and political contracts between families (Coontz, 2005). Often it wasn't the two people getting married who were making the choice to marry; it was their parents, community elders, clergy or politicians. That today two people choose to get married on the basis of the fact that they love each other is a societal conversation that has been around only since the late seventeen hundreds, just over two hundred years ago.

Marriage as a Conversation for Individual Choice. The Age of Enlightenment in the seventeenth and eighteenth centuries influenced relations between men and women in radical ways. Ideals such as individual liberty, freedom of speech and equality began to shape people's conception of marriage. In Western Europe and America, marriage was being redefined as an inalienable choice between a man and a woman. This freedom to choose whom one could marry was an utterly new idea. It ushered in a new realm of personal responsibility for the state of marriage. One could argue that without fundamental free will or the choice to marry, a person or a couple had no real sense of responsibility for the quality of one's marriage. Prior to this time, two people could live in a state of matrimony, but pay little attention to the health of their relationship. For thousands of years, a husband wielded great power in marriage, meting out punishment to his disobeying wife, owning all the property in the family, including his wife's possessions, and making the family's decisions unilaterally. There was little equality between the sexes, no real freedom of speech or any real focus on the quality of one's marriage. All this began to change during the Age of Enlightenment.

Coontz (2005) writes that for the first time in thousands of years, men and women now could choose whom they would marry. This choice was a personal and a private choice that replaced arranged marriage as a necessary economic or political tradition. The rise of the market economy during the late eighteenth and early nineteenth centuries changed the fundamental ideas around gender roles in marriage. Men were freed from their families to earn a living and the husband was now seen as the person in the family who was the main provider and responsible for the economic well-being of the family. A wife's role was to set moral standards and attend to the emotional needs of the family. Married couples set up their own households and their homes became places of refuge from their work and community responsibilities. The emotional climate in the home began to be an important factor in the health and well-being of one's marriage.

Marriage as a Conversation for Lifelong Love. With men and women now being able to choose whom they would marry, another new and very radical idea began to take hold. Couples began to marry for one simple little reason: They loved each other. While the freedom to choose one's mate in marriage created a new sense of responsibility for spouses to have their marriage work on their own terms, marrying on the basis of love created a completely new challenge for couples. For a marriage to be successful, a couple was now challenged with keeping their connection alive over time and with experiencing an enduring love for each other. Coontz (2005) writes that as soon as marriage became a choice between two people on the basis of love, the very foundation of marriage became more fragile. Almost as soon as couples had the freedom to marry on the basis of love, the movement to create a legal system that allowed divorce on the basis of the loss of love was born (Coontz, 2005). Choosing to stay married long after their original vows and keeping their experience of love, affection and connection alive for years to come were both now squarely the couple's job.

Also, without the economic and political contracts between families in force, what would make a couple's marriage real in the eyes of the community? Getting married in a church with the ceremony officiated by a priest or minister and having that marriage be licensed by the state, as it is in the United States, are relatively new developments in the history of marriage (Coontz, 2005). While not being arranged for economic or political purposes, a marriage now had to be sanctified by somebody who had the power granted by the state or religious institution to legitimize one's marriage. And just as important, a marriage had to be witnessed and recognized by a community of people, even if that community of people was only one person. Through these institutional practices, a marriage between two people who loved each other and made the choice to get married now had a process by which their marriage became real in the eyes of the community. A couple's marriage was now a formal and legal union based on the freedom to choose and self-proclaimed love.

In earlier centuries, relationships between men and women were based more on power, force and authority, rather than reason, justice or equality. But by the beginning of the nineteenth century, marriage was being shaped by new societal conversations: Individuals were free to choose their mate, they could marry on the basis of love and marriage was a formal union between a man and a woman recognized by the state as real and legitimate. At the same time, another very radical conversation was also having a great impact on the relationship between the sexes and on the institution of marriage—the idea of equality.

Marriage as a Conversation for Equality. The social conversation that men and women are equal under the law has been evolving in the United States over the last two hundred years. Radical changes occurred in the 1970s that put men and women on a more equal footing in marriage. In 1972, the Equal Rights Amendment (ERA), a proposed amendment to the United States Constitution, was passed in both houses of Congress, but has never been ratified by the prerequisite two thirds of state legislatures. Efforts to revive the ERA over the years, however, have proved fruitless.

Since the 1970s, marriage has been in the process of being redefined in many households on the basis of true equality. Many wives and a fewer number of husbands have attempted to establish more equitable arrangements at home around accountability for household and parental responsibilities. When they were married in 1972, neither Jeanne nor Richard was interested in a conventional marriage. They each had careers, valued their free time and felt that the traditional distribution of responsibilities at home didn't seem equitable to them. Jeanne and Richard, who participated in my Partners in Living couples course, shared this with me.

Very early in our marriage we had a conversation about how we could equally assume responsibility for household chores. We both valued a clean and neat home and wanted to get all our errands and chores done in a way that was smooth and didn't involve weekly squabbles about whose job was what and didn't cause resentment stemming from one of us spending more time on housework than the other. We were both working in demanding, full-time jobs, and we wanted to be able to each have an equal amount of leisure time.

The answer was very simple. We divided the work by time, not roles, with the goal of having equal time for each of us for work and equal time for each of us for play. So a typical Saturday morning would involve dividing up the weekly chores of cleaning the bathrooms, vacuuming, dusting, etc. so that before noon we were both finished and the house was clean. During the week, I did most of the cooking and Richard usually did the dishes. Other chores and errands were handled the same way.

Over the years with the arrival of our children and other changes in our lives we have tried to maintain the principle of "equal work, equal play." When Richard was working full time and I was home for a few years full time with the kids, our responsibilities changed. When I returned to work, things shifted again. Now, even as we are both retired, we are still trying to live by the same principle.

Steil (1997), who examined the relationship of marital equality to the well-being of husbands and wives, found that from the 1970s to the 1990s, women's roles expanded dramatically whereas men's roles had not. By the early 1990s, wives were still responsible for most of the childcare and household responsibilities in comparison to that of their husbands. While the state and federal laws around marital equality were changing rapidly, the economic, social and cultural conversations that determined men and women's actual roles in society have been slower to change.

Steil (1997) expressed his vision of the potential benefits of marital equality for husbands, wives and their relationship this way:

> In equal relationships, men have the opportunity to relinquish the mantle of total economic responsibility and family dependency, to involve themselves in parenting, and to more fully express their emotional and nurturing selves. Women have the opportunity to develop themselves professionally, develop a sense of self independent of their husband and their children, and achieve economic independence and higher self-esteem (Gilbert & Rachlin, 1987). Finally, men and women together have the opportunity to be part of more intimate relationships based on mutual reliance and respect that is so important to a satisfying relationship and to both husbands' and wives' well-being (p. 115).

Since the 1970s, many husbands and wives have been reformulating ways in which they can create their marriages in the spirit of equality, fairness and choice.

Marriage as a Conversation for Self-development and Personal Growth. One of the ideals in a partnership marriage today is that one can fulfill one's commitment to self-expression, personal growth and life goals inside of marriage. Most couples recognize that they must continually grow and develop throughout their life together or their marriage will stagnate. That, however, requires a commitment from both partners to support each other's personal and professional growth as well as that of their relationship and their marriage. Today, this is a major challenge in creating a fulfilling marriage over a lifetime.

Starting in the 1960s and spanning the latter half of the twentieth century, new views of human potential were taking root across the American landscape. In the field of developmental psychology, the study of life span development took hold in the 1980s as psychologists, biologists and gerontologists became interested in the study of individual development from conception into old age (Baltes, Staudinger, & Lindenberger, 1999). Previously, particularly in America, the emphasis of developmental study was on child psychology and child development. The core assumption that human development and growth stops around eighteen to twenty-one years of age gave way to the view that human beings continue to develop into adulthood and even well into their twilight years (Baltes, 1997). This new emphasis contributed to people thinking about their own personal and professional development across their entire life span.

Coinciding with shifts in academic views of human development, many people in the 1970s were awakening to their own self-development through their participation in the new human potential movement. The human potential movement that began in the early 1960s and grew throughout the latter half of the twentieth century spawned new thinking about the untapped potential in all people. New views of human potential suggested that through personal development and awareness, people could shift the quality of their life dramatically, be creative, find happiness and achieve fulfillment. This movement had its beginnings in 1962 at the Esalen Institute, which was one of the first centers to study human potential. Many therapists in the late 1960s and 70s, including Frits Perls, Virginia Satir and Carl Rogers, began to turn their attention to holistic, humanistic and person-centered health approaches to work with people, rather than just the study and treatment of pathology.

Also in the 1970s, weekend self-empowerment programs like the est training, Actualizations and Lifespring were popular on the West Coast and grew rapidly throughout the United States. In addition, the self-help industry exploded with books, manuals and videotapes being released into the marketplace at a dizzying rate, focused on self-development topics ranging from relationship advice, healthy eating, and personal training to twelve-step support, motivational speaking and advice on how to help you be more organized and manage your time effectively. The American culture became permeated with the value and belief that through self-improvement and growth every human being could design fulfilling lives, accomplish their goals, and achieve joy and happiness. Even in the mega-churches, such as those of Joel Osteen and Rick Warren in the Midwest, marriage has oriented around an emphasis on self-development and fulfillment of the individual. Cherlin (2009) suggests that religions today encourage marriage, but also promote spiritual and personal growth.

Finally, in the latter part of the twentieth century, the professional coaching industry began to blossom. Today, there are numerous coaching training programs throughout the country turning out hundreds of coaches each year trained to support people in almost every conceivable area of their lives, including weight control, life planning, personal fulfillment, relationship skills, productivity, leadership and team building.

This emerging belief that individuals continue to develop themselves across a lifetime combined with the values of equality and equity in relationships has put new pressures on marriage to be a vehicle for personal fulfillment for *both* individuals. A model of partnership in marriage resolves the seemingly inherent conflict between the value of marriage and the value of individualism that Cherlin (2009) has distinguished in the American culture. *Creating a partnership marriage requires the couple to focus on their growth and development as individuals as well as on the fulfillment of their relationship.* Partnership marriage works for "me, you and us." Each individual's personal growth and development is expressed, nurtured and supported by one's marriage and, thus, their marriage also grows and develops. One's personal dreams and fulfillment do not have to be sacrificed for the sake of one's partnership. Also, partnership in one's marriage does not have to be sacrificed for the sake of one's individualism.

Marriage as a Conversation for Being a Right of All People. Cherlin (2009) writes that the AIDS epidemic among gay and lesbian individuals in the 1980s highlighted the disparity between the rights and privileges of heterosexual and homosexual citizens in the United States. Gay partners of people who were sick with AIDS couldn't get visiting privileges, authorize treatment for their loved ones, buy health insurance coverage for their partner or make funeral arrangements. By the 1990s, gays and lesbians began to organize and mobilize state by state to be able to legally marry each other, a right enjoyed by *every* heterosexual person in the United States.

In the last twenty years, a vast number of Americans now see marriage as a right for all people, regardless of sexual orientation. It is only a matter of time before marriage rights will be extended to all same-sex couples. In 2010, a federal court in Massachusetts ruled as unconstitutional a 1996 law passed by Congress, called the Defense of Marriage Act (DOMA), which prevented the federal government from recognizing same-sex marriage. Most recently, the United States Supreme Court struck down DOMA, but upheld that part of the law not requiring states to recognize same-sex marriage licenses from other states. The societal conversation for marriage as a legal right for all people is fully underway and is likely to have important ramifications for years to come.

In the last three hundred years, societal conversations have transformed the institution of marriage for every American. Today, we take for granted that you have the right to choose your lifelong marital mate. No one else can make that choice for you. Also, culturally, we know that the vast majority of couples who do marry do so on the basis that they love each other and that their commitment to marriage requires a love that lasts a lifetime. Today, increasingly, two persons who join in wedlock conceive of themselves as true equals, in other words, as having an equal and equitable contribution to the health and vitality of their marriage. Also, both individuals, more than any time in history, see their marriage as an arrangement that must allow for the personal growth not only of each person but also of the couple's relationship. And finally, more and more Americans are recognizing that marriage is a right that should be legally extended to every citizen, regardless of sexual orientation. These societal conversations have shaped the institution of marriage, as we know it today.

Partnership: A Missing Conversation for Marriage?

When I go into bookstores and pick up books on marriage, I often go right to the index to see if I can find the word "partnership." It always surprises me when I can't find it listed. I also occasionally search the Internet for "partnership." What I get are hundreds of links to websites for domestic partnerships, non-profit organizations or business partnerships. If you are partners, you must either be gay or lesbian, you must be working for a non-profit or you must be building a business together! I don't see many websites concerned with partnership in marriage. I recently bought the URL www.thepartnershipmarriage.com, and was completely surprised that it was available. The idea that marriage is fundamentally a lifelong conversation for creating a fulfilling and enduring partnership seems to be missing in the national discourse!

Fowers (2000) writes that a great myth about marriage today is that marriage itself will make us happy or meet all of our emotional needs. He suggests that happiness is no longer the main purpose of marriage. When happiness or emotional gratification can't be reliably achieved in marriage, people more often than not give up and end their marriage in divorce. Fowers (2000) suggests that happiness and emotional gratification may be an important by-product, but they are not the purpose of marriage. He posits that a strong marriage is built on a shared vision of the future, shared sacrifices and teamwork around the mundane tasks of living together. He suggests that couples who are committed to a strong marriage ultimately shift their focus from emotional gratification to the quality of their partnership in life.

Partnership is a natural expression of your marriage if you and your spouse see yourselves as being responsible for the choice you made to get married in the first place. Being responsible for that choice forges a sense of personal commitment for the health and vitality of your marriage.

Partnership is a passionate demonstration of your love for each other if you understand that your love is freely given and shared in your marriage. If you see yourselves as partners in life, you will be responsible for keeping the love and respect you have for each other alive over the long haul.

Partnership is a powerful context for your marriage if you view yourselves as equal human beings with the same rights and opportunities to pursue your aspirations in life. If you hold each other as equals in life, you will also honor each other's commitments and work together to create a life where your roles and responsibilities are equitable. If those roles and responsibilities are not fairly distributed, you will work out your household arrangements so that both of you feel that your contributions are fair and appreciated by each other.

Partnership is a valuable perspective for viewing your marriage if you are committed to each other in fulfilling your goals, individually and collectively. If you are committed to partnership in your marriage, you will grant each other authorship or agency to pursue what is important to you individually while also pursuing your shared dreams.

And finally, partnership is a way of being for any two people, regardless of sexual orientation, who have the extraordinary privilege to marry and the opportunity to create a long and happy life together. A partnership marriage ultimately is created over the course of many conversations in which you and your spouse honor the values that are important to you, fulfill your vision for a shared life, master life's challenges together and sustain an enduring love for each other.

The kinds of conversations that you have in your relationship have great power in determining whether your marriage will endure, be fulfilling and be lifelong or whether your marriage will head toward divorce or, even worse, last over time but be lifeless, stagnant and unhappy. A partnership marriage in this respect is not for faint of heart. It takes everything you have.

Chapter

3

THE POWER OF CONVERSATION
IN MARRIAGE

"Ultimately the bond of all companionship, whether in marriage or in friendship, is conversation, and conversation must have a common basis..."

–Oscar Wilde

If you are married or in a long-term committed relationship with your partner, you will express all kinds of feelings, viewpoints, opinions, judgments and ideas in conversation with each other over a lifetime. Your conversations will, at times, be creative, productive and affirming and other times may be reactive, static and conflicting. You will exchange different viewpoints, share what is going on in your lives, solve issues, create a vision for the future and make plans of action. You will express what is working and not working for each of you in your marriage. You will share what you like and don't like, what you appreciate and don't appreciate and what you're committed to and not committed to. You may find things that are wrong with each other and blame each other. You may argue and even stop talking to each other for long periods of time. You will have conversations that express your partnership on a daily basis or that argue for "the way that it is and always will be" in your marriage. You will have conversations that promote the health and vitality of your marriage or that defend its status quo.

Consider for a moment that it is the nature of your conversations that determines the quality, the vibrancy and the vitality of your marriage. Today, for you to have an enduring and fulfilling marriage, you must learn to be effective in having all kinds of conversations. *The kinds of conversations that you and your spouse routinely engage in over time have a profound impact on what is possible in your marriage and on the effectiveness of your partnership. The quality of your conversations shapes your experience of fulfillment in your life together and your expression of partnership in your marriage.*

Reactive Conversations: The World from *My* Point of View

David Bohm (1996) in his treatise on dialogue examines the nature of communication between people. He suggests that one way to think about communication is that it is used to express information, points or view, or opinions in a unidirectional way. One person has a specific idea and wants to convey his ideas to others. In such communication, an individual is solely concerned with his ideas being heard. In other words, the person has an attachment to his own point of view and is not necessarily interested in considering different ideas, opinions or viewpoints. If others don't agree with his idea(s), he may defend his point of view and fail to connect in a meaningful way with his listeners.

You could say that the person communicating this way has a lack of awareness of his listener's point of view. I have been at many cocktail parties where someone will say something, then someone else will say something unrelated to what the person just said. The two people are stating their points of view without any connection or commitment to having a real conversation with a joint focus. Such conversations are reactive, static and identity-driven, in which each person is more interested in expressing their point of view than in connecting with another. Martha and I do this sometimes.

I'll be talking to her about one topic; she'll be talking to me about another. Then we'll notice that we're not having a conversation at all. We each just want the other to hear what we are saying.

Bohm (1996) distinguishes discussion from true dialogue. The word discussion has the same root word as concussion or percussion, originating from the Latin word, *percutere*, which means, "to strike forcibly." In a discussion, individuals express their own points of view and bat their ideas back and forth. At best, they are attempting to come to some agreement, but in actuality each person is attempting to dominate others with their opinions or perspectives. The idea is to win or win over others to one's own point of view. Bohm (1996) suggests that, in this kind of conversation, the point of the interaction is to win. In such conversations, individuals are focused on the content of what they are saying, on their own thoughts and opinions, and on defending them against disagreement, often to the detriment of the quality of the relationship with the person with whom they are conversing. These kinds of conversations are essentially reactive and don't tend to create anything new. Instead, they are focused on winning and losing.

Such reactive conversations and expressions of opinion are based in the past and tend to describe the way life is. These are conversations in which people talk *about* life. Couples will talk about the way their marriage is. Husbands talk about their wives or wives talk about their husbands. Gossip, complaints, judgments, criticism, accusation and blame are all manifestations of conversations about another, a relationship, marriage or some aspect of life. The person speaking often appears to want to be heard. More accurately, though, the individual wants to be right and to justify their point of view.

When you and your spouse are talking about some aspect of your relationship, you may relate to each other as if you are each an observer giving your perspective on its status quo. It's as if you are standing outside your relationship, looking at it through a window and describing what you each see from your own vantage point. You each become observers judging and describing "the way that it is" in your relationship. The subject of your conversation can take on the quality of a static condition or of a fixed reality. In such conversations, you may have a sense that "nothing can be done," which leaves you and your partner feeling powerless and resigned.

A conversation about your life and relationship is often focused on what has happened in the past. Such a conversation is characterized by a description of what happened and by offering an explanation for how it occurred. You tend to give reasons why it happened, give opinions about what should have happened or how it could have been different. Such conversations are characterized by judgments, assessments and evaluations of good and bad or of right and wrong. In these kinds of conversations, you tend to speak as if neither of you is responsible for what's going on in your marriage, describing what's happening from the safe sanctuary of "outside" the relationship.

It is not unlike spectators at a baseball game. Spectators have a lot to say at the game, but none of it really makes any difference to the play of the game on the field. The spectators sit in the stands and talk about what is happening in the baseball game. All kinds of conversations occur in the stands of a baseball game, such as yelling, complaining, blaming, explaining, predicting, hoping or cheering, but all of it has little to do with what is actually happening in the game itself. When you are engaged in assessing each other, it is as if you both have just gone up into the stands of your relationship to report on or react to your partner. In the stands of a relationship, you may give pronouncements (giving "you" messages, personalizing the problem, or blaming the other person), opinions (asserting the way it is) and judgments (labeling and making generalizations) in which you are attached to being right and making each other or something in your relationship wrong. If you stay in the stands of your relationship, neither of you may feel that you have the ability to impact the "play of the game," have effective interactions or reach mutually satisfying outcomes in your relationship.

If you engage in these kinds of conversations, you will, in effect, keep re-creating the status quo and experience little hope for change or for something new. You already know how it's going to be and feel that whatever you do won't make anything different or better. In such conversations, you both may feel that you can't navigate the course of your relationship in the way that could make a real difference for your marriage. A multitude of judgments, opinions and attitudes prevail and reinforce the way that "it is," defend points of view, explain what happened and limit what's possible in your future.

If you and your spouse regularly engage in such conversations about your marriage, you will have difficulty experiencing the fullness of your lives together. You will have difficulty listening to each other and understanding each other. You may find it difficult to understand each other's experience, point of view or what is important to each other. Something always seems wrong. A sense of being profoundly connected is absent. Sharing a rich emotional life, an expression of partnership and an ability to create your lives together are unavailable.

Reactive conversations about your life and relationship allow for no genuine expressions of feelings, of shared experience or of appreciation for what each of you contributes to the partnership. It can be difficult to understand each other, see what is really happening in your relationship or discern what is working and what is not working in your life. It can be challenging for you to create any new perspective or shift your point of view to give you greater freedom and power in dealing with what's going on in your lives. And finally, effectively resolving conflicts, issues, dilemmas and problems is very difficult. The mood in your relationship may be one of quiet resignation, powerlessness and cynicism.

Understanding the nature of conversation can have an impact on what is actually possible in your marriage over time. How would the quality of your relationship be enhanced if you learned ways to converse with each other that allowed you both to be fully self-expressed? What would be possible for you, as a couple, if you were able to develop the tools to have conversations to design your life together and to enhance the quality of your marriage? Such an alteration in the nature of your conversations with each other could have an extraordinary and lasting impact of your experience of partnership.

Creative Conversations: A World from *Our* Point of View

Bohm (1996) suggests that a creative conversation or dialogue involves two or more people who are interested in understanding each other rather than being right or defending their points of view. The essential nature of dialogue is that it is an exchange or communication of ideas, feelings or perspectives where you and your spouse are interested in listening to and understanding each other. In dialogue, Bohm (1996) suggests you share ideas and thoughts with each other, listen for what is being expressed and create something new in the conversation.

In such conversations, it is important that you pay attention to the process of your communication as well as the content of what you are saying. It is, in fact, the quality of your connection that is most important. In his research with over 2,000 couples, John Gottman (1994) studied the patterns of interaction and the "emotional ecology" of marital relationships. He discovered that, in stable and healthy marriages, couples engaged in approximately five positive interactions to every one negative interaction. He called this finding the "magic ratio" and found it to be predictive of marital relationships that were characterized by love and respect. These couples tended to show concern and caring for each other, affection toward one another and interest in nurturing the connection between them.

He found that conflict was not necessarily harmful to a marriage as long as couples could engage in what he calls repair mechanisms, where they are able to restore their loving connection with each other. Anger and disagreement were found to be healthy for one's marriage if the couple had sound ways to resolve issues and solve problems as they arose.

One of the most interesting findings was that couples who could focus on *how they were interacting* with each other when they were in conflict had much better success in resolving their issues without hurting their relationship. Right in the middle of their argument, one person might request to be heard by their partner or to be able to finish what they were saying without being interrupted. Also, these couples would stop to comment on what was happening in their interaction or they would let their partner know that they were still listening.

Couples who have a healthy emotional ecology in their marriage are able to stay focused both on the conversation at hand and manage the emotional sphere between them. They are able to simultaneously attend to the content *and* the process of their interactions. In other words, such couples are able to pay attention to the quality of their relationship with each other, even when their conversation gets a bit heated or difficult.

In creative conversations, couples have a commitment to win-win or to their relationship winning. Bohm (1996) writes that when conversations are generative, no one person is attempting to win or dominate the conversation; the idea is to have a conversation that is mutually satisfying to both individuals. When one person wins, both people win. Each person takes care to understand the other and to listen for what new understanding is emerging in the conversation. Neither person is attempting to be right or have his or her viewpoint prevail. In conversations that are creative in nature, both persons are usually aware that their viewpoints are just that: They are points of view. Both persons are more committed to a mutually satisfying outcome for their relationship than being right about their opinion or viewpoint. It is difficult and nearly impossible to have the experience of loving and caring connection with your spouse when one of you has to be right about your point of view. Being unattached to your own point of view allows you to hear and understand other points of view. In a creative conversation, the two of you are able converse with one another and think together without being attached to your points of view.

When I reflect on all the conversations Martha and I have had over the years, I can see that many of them have been reactive in nature when we have argued, disagreed and felt like we had to defend our cherished points of view. At these times, we were jockeying for some position of advantage over each other. At many other times, though, our conversations have been creative and generative when we felt connected and cared for. Whether we are solving a problem, negotiating something with each other, sharing experiences, planning a trip or envisioning a future, if our conversation is creative, we are nurturing the quality of our marriage.

When you have a conversation that nurtures your marriage, you stand together for the growth, health and fulfillment of your partnership. You have a profound sense that you are the authors of your own destiny. You both experience being on the same playing field of life. You are "in the game" together, each recognizing the other as a teammate. You each recognize that your relationship, your partnership and your experience of your life are *in your hands*. How you play together in the game of life makes all the difference. You see your partnership as created in conversation and in action. You understand the importance of setting aside time to speak with each other about what is important to you, about your future and about plans for committed action to bring into reality the vision of your future. You recognize that creating vision without taking action is just hopeful thinking and taking action without a clear plan guided by a sense of what is possible is ineffective and shortsighted.

When you are committed to partnership in your marriage, you learn to align yourselves with your values and what is important to you. You share your dreams with each other and what you see is possible for your marriage. In such conversations, you create a safe and magical space where you can say what you envision without fear of limitation, judgment, disagreement or conflict. Each of you has the freedom to share what images of the future you see. "I'd love us to have three children." "I want to buy an old colonial house with a large front porch and a backyard with a swimming pool." "I am committed to going back to graduate school." "I see a future in which we take a two-month, around-the-world tour visiting countries on every continent." "I am going to own and drive a BMW Roadster by the time I am sixty years old." Inventing a vision for your future together and being in alignment around what is important generates a trust and belief in the long-term durability of your marriage.

Conversations about what happened in the past can also powerfully express the quality of your marriage. Stories about what has happened in the past can be a rich source of shared memories, images and emotions for your relationship. You can see what you have learned together, what you have risked together, where you have failed and what you have accomplished. Your shared past becomes a source of rich meaning for you. Bringing the past alive by sharing it with others is a powerful way that you can create and honor your partnership. In addition, the past or everything that has happened in your marriage up to the present moment can be experienced as being on track to fulfilling the future you want for your lives. At that moment, you experience yourselves as being in the right moment on a long journey together.

This ability to share powerfully about the past occurs when you learn to have conversations for completion and acceptance. To be complete with something is to experience satisfying closure. When you are able accept each other, you experience wholeness in your relationship. If being in a healthy marriage were like a riding on an old western stagecoach with four large wheels with wooden spokes, you would continuously be tending to the soundness and health of all those spokes. The spokes in each wheel are integral to stability and functioning of the wheels. When you are not honoring what you say is important in your marriage, it is as if you have taken your attention off the integrity of spokes of your relationship. As a result, the spokes (and wheels) of your marriage will begin to fall apart and the vitality of your relationship will begin to suffer. Like a stagecoach, you might find yourselves and your relationship in a ditch.

When resolving issues or difficulties with each other in partnership, you grant space for each other's feelings and emotions. Feelings are viewed as natural and are included in the context of the relationship. Feelings are normalized and embraced. They are validated and acknowledged. In this way, you learn to trust each other's internal world and experience. By validating each other, you provide safety for each other when talking about difficult issues. Such safety allows you to take risks with each other.

You recognize that for your marriage to be vibrant, loving and fulfilling, both of you must support each other's long-term success and happiness. You recognize that when one person feels that he or she is not happy in the relationship, you both are suffering and your partnership suffers as well. You learn to cease engaging in the patterns of interaction that create suffering in your relationship and interact in ways that promote the well-being of each other and your marriage.

When problems or issues arise in your interactions with each other, it is particularly effective for you to examine exactly what's happening by separating the facts of what's going on from your interpretations of what happened. In this way, you can deal responsibly with the circumstances. You can then look at your intention or commitment in the matter, discern what is working and not working and see what is missing that you can address. Using the stagecoach metaphor, you can attend to a spoke in your marriage that may be missing or broken. You can then discern the action required to resolve your difficulty. Taking such action might be to establish the facts of what happened, apologize, forgive one another and/or make a new promise.

One of the most powerful conversations you can have is a conversation for creating a context for your relationship. A context is a shared framework or perspective that gives you both a way to view and relate to your life circumstances. A couple who can invent an empowering context for their marriage has a very powerful way to deal with whatever circumstances life presents them. An example of a shared context might be "Our life is an adventure and we will make it work." Another powerful way you can deal with dilemmas, issues and problems is to adopt the framework that "there is nothing wrong" with each other, your relationship or with the circumstances with which you are dealing. Rather than looking at who is right or who is wrong in the situation, you both can look at what is working and what is not working against the backdrop of what you are committed to. Creating a shared empowering perspective of life shapes the way you relate to your circumstances, listen for what is possible and view the opportunities in front of you. You are able to take action that is coordinated and effective.

Support on the playing field of your lives most frequently comes in the form of making requests and promises of each other. You learn to have your attention on cooperation, teamwork and taking the appropriate action. "Will you get the dry cleaning tomorrow before 10:00 AM?" "I will schedule a car tune-up in the afternoon after 2:00 PM." "Let's meet to discuss our finances tonight at 8:00 PM." Committing to plan, taking action and reviewing how things are going all represent the non-stop world for couples in partnership. When you become masterful at making requests and promises with each other, you become skilled at creating partnership in your lives. Effective action is a continual expression of your active commitment to each other. When requests are not made or promises broken, the dancing and the coordination in your partnership can become awkward and ineffective.

Lastly, being in partnership also means you also stop "doing" and take the time to be with each other. You continually regenerate your relationship by scheduling time with one another to enjoy and appreciate your relationship. Dating over the life span is an expression of this commitment. Dating allows you to be with each other, to honor each other and to replenish your relationship. This becomes a lifelong commitment.

Being in a partnership marriage allows for two people to bear witness to each other's lives over a very long period of time. When you are committed to partnership, you continually see each other's strengths, weaknesses, successes, failures, accomplishments, fears, wants, dreams and joys. You stand for each other's goodness and greatness. You witness the magnificence of each other and of your relationship. You are partners on the same field of life engaged in conversations to create life and to nurture the quality of your marriage. You engage in conversations for wholeness, for healing, for sharing, for growth, for transformation, for fulfillment and for profound love.

Marriage as a Conversation for Partnership

In the previous chapter, I suggested that partnership seems to be missing in the national discourse around marriage. Consider that marriage is a lifelong conversation *for* partnership in which you are focused on the quality of your relationship and the life you are building together. Partnership requires that you see yourselves as equals who want to learn and grow and to participate together in fulfilling your dreams. Here comes the harder part—learning and using the conversational tools to create partnership in your marriage. In this book, I will give you and your spouse these tools with which you can design your marriage, develop empowering perspectives together and transform ways of being together that can enhance your experience of being partners each and every day.

To be partners in life, I recommend that you adopt the framework that you, as individuals, and your relationship are whole, imaginative, competent and enterprising in dealing with circumstances in life. Holding another person as "creative, resourceful and whole" is a central cornerstone of the paradigm for a coaching relationship developed by Whitworth, Kimsey-House, & Sandahl (1998). In this framework, each of you hold yourself as creative and capable of being, doing and having whatever you are willing to commit yourself to. You each view yourself as the "author" of your lives and your relationship. You hold yourselves as intrinsically whole people. There is nothing wrong and nothing to be fixed.

For you both to intentionally adopt the perspective that there is nothing inherently wrong with each other or your relationship is a bold and courageous act. Consciously holding each other as whole and your marriage as healthy allows you to share an extraordinary life together over the long term. Partnership becomes a powerful context for your lives.

This context becomes the container in which your marriage is held and gives meaning to all the content and the "stuff" in your lives. Each of you creates this perspective by declaring: "I unconditionally accept you, our relationship and our marriage as whole and complete." By making such a declaration, you each experience being free to be naturally self-expressed, to have a relationship that is whole and to embrace the viewpoint that there is nothing inherently wrong with your marriage. It is a perspective from which you can create your lives and to which you can return when life is not working as well as you would like it to.

This perspective of partnership for your marriage allows you both to shift from perceiving problems as flaws in your relationship to opportunities for a collaborative inquiry and effective action. Areas that are not working in your marriage are viewed as normal occurrences that require you to take the time to get into communication with each other and have a conversation. When you operate from mutual acceptance of each other and your relationship, you are able to powerfully focus on the problem or issue at hand and avoid assessing the issue as a weakness in your marriage.

When you are committed to partnership in your marriage, you are always looking to move your lives and your relationship forward in the direction of workability. All areas of your life and your relationship can be examined and there is nothing too small or seemingly insignificant to talk about. Some of the most valuable lessons in living together can be found in discussing such things as how to open a tuna fish can, who is going to take the package to the post office or who is going to pick up the take-out dinner for that evening. Every feeling, point of view, opinion or judgment about something is included in your relationship. Political interests, recreational preferences, the management of money, sexual expressiveness, household roles and responsibilities and parenting styles all become important in the context of a partnership marriage.

If you have differing political viewpoints, standards of cleanliness or sexual interests, you learn to discuss and resolve your differences directly with each other. By including and effectively dealing with all that is in your marriage, there is nothing that "should or should not belong" in your relationship. You learn to deal with what is actually occurring in your marriage and in your lives. When you can't talk about something that at least one of you feels is important, the freedom of self-expression in your relationship diminishes. Granting the permission to talk about anything, no matter how important or seemingly insignificant, is a gift that you give each other.

By consciously adopting the framework that everything in your marriage is potentially important, you can learn to embrace all of life as you learn to live together. Rather than not talking about things or avoiding some subjects, each of you can say what you need to say without your partner minimizing its importance. If you can discuss anything, you can keep returning to the experience of wholeness without having some issue, no matter how big or small, get in the way of that experience. Inside this context everything in life becomes "grist for the mill" for creating partnership.

Whitworth, Kimsey-House, and Sandahl (1998) wrote that a life that is fulfilling is a valued life. A model of partnership in marriage starts with the premise that every married couple has their own unique expression of what they value. The degree to which couples honor their values impacts their experience of what's possible for them, their expression of partnership and their passion for their marriage. What do I mean by possibility, partnership and passion?

Possibility. In a partnership marriage you are able to create a vision for your lives together and a future that is both possible and gives you a sense of direction and purpose. You are able to invent a desired future and to work as a team together to have that vision realized. Your vision is a joint vision, in which you have a shared stake in the quality of your lives and real power in working together. Examples of such declarative statements are: "We are committed to being loving and generous with each other." "We are a stand for peace and harmony in relationships with others." "We declare that we are committed partners dedicated to creating a life filled with an adventure, wonder and miracles."

Such declarations express your commitment to what you hold dear in your relationship. One of the most intimate activities you can engage in is having a conversation for the vision of your partnership and for your future. Permission to dream, sharing hopes and desires, expressing support for each other's growth and development, brainstorming ideas and inventing the future together are all expressions of such a shared vision. This kind of sharing can be very intimate and loving.

Partnership: Partnership is more than just having a vision together. It also requires the sharing of all the day-to-day, logistical, how-are-we-going-to-handle-everything-we've-got-to-do kinds of commitments, activities and projects in life. As partners you must sort out who is going to do what and when. Like a pair of jugglers, throwing bowling pins back and forth to each other or like two trapeze artists, flying through the air, catching each other fifty feet above the circus ring, you learn to work together effectively and in a coordinated way. When there is effective communication, action and coordination, balls don't get dropped and people do not fall into the net below. Successful coordination and aligned activity create a sense of trust, feelings of satisfaction and an expression of real competence. You cooperate with each other and things get accomplished!

The experience of partnership is challenged when your communication breaks down and your coordinated activity falters. When this occurs, if you are committed to partnership, you will examine and communicate what you are committed to. Effectiveness is enhanced by focusing on what is working and not working rather than who is wrong or who is to blame. The way you deal with issues, problems and breakdowns is an expression of your commitment to being partners.

Passion: When you are committed to living passionately, you give each other the permission to live lives you both love. You won't settle for anything less. You are aware of the wonderful opportunity of sharing an enduring, fulfilling life together.

In today's world, there are many influences, demands, requirements, concerns, issues, etc. that compete for your attention. It is easy to give up and to say, "Our dreams are not that important" or "What fulfills us must be put on hold." When you commit yourselves to partnership, you say "no" to resignation, cynicism and the status quo. You say "no" to your fears and your self-limiting beliefs. You say "no" to helplessness and hopelessness. When you are committed to creating a partnership marriage, you say "yes" to living lives you love and to loving the life you share. You continually express a strong enthusiasm for each other and for building and sharing your lives together.

Emerging Conversations of Partnership Marriage

The marriage literature is replete with models of marriage as a series of stages through which a couple fulfills their marital journey (Harrar & DeMaria, 2007). Many of these stage models are strikingly similar. In the next six chapters, I outline six distinct phases of marriage. I do not, however, attempt to create a new stage model, per se; rather, I focus on delineating the marital commitments and kinds of conversations that are central to each phase of marriage. As your marriage grows and matures with each phase, you deepen your commitment to each other and to your life together. Within each phase of marriage, you also engage in important conversations upon which the quality of your marriage is built. *At each phase in the development of a long-term marital partnership, you invest in a new promise and possibility for your marriage.*

It is well documented that how well a couple is able communicate with each other is critical to the long-term success of their marriage (Markman, Stanley & Blumberg, 2001). Having effective conversations for planning, negotiating, problem-solving, resolving conflict, being intimate with each other, etc. that build a happy and healthy marriage takes considerable time, energy and attention (Marano, 2006). Understanding the work required in each marital stage can give you a roadmap for dealing with the myriad of issues and challenges that present themselves at different times along your life's path (Harrar and DeMaria, 2007).

Understanding the essential conversations at each phase of marriage can also give you access to transforming how you view your marriage over the long haul and how you relate to each other, each and every day. By learning to successfully engage in the central conversations at each phase on that journey, you both grow individually and are able to nurture the quality of your relationship. The kinds of conversations you are able have at one stage stand on the success you have had in conversations at previous stages and also set the foundation for your being able to have important conversations in subsequent phases of your marriage.

Mastery in the foundational conversations in a marriage is not completely linear; it may also be cyclical. When you are having difficulty in one phase of your marriage, you may need to re-visit conversations with which you have become proficient at previous times. For example, in the first years of their relationship, a couple has many conversations to get to know each other and connect in very important ways. Later, when the couple is married and living together, if they begin to argue about their roles and responsibilities to the detriment of their sense of teamwork and daily workability, they may need to reconnect around what's important to them. Returning to conversations that connect them to their values may provide the necessary foundation for them to be able to negotiate their roles and household tasks effectively and to create a sense of "We are on the same team."

In Chapters 4 through 9, I present a model of partnership marriage in which the key conversations in six phases of marriage become building blocks for creating a life you love. You and your spouse can learn, can practice and be coached in having many kinds of conversations that have a profound impact on what is possible in your lives and on the quality of your marriage. It is the premise of this book that marriage is fundamentally a network of conversations *for* lifelong partnership. The conversations for each phase presented in the following chapters are designed to give you and your partner access to building an enduring and fulfilling partnership marriage.

Chapter

4

FALLING INTO US

CONVERSATIONS FOR CONNECTION, COMMITMENT AND COUPLE-NESS

"Happy marriages are based on a deep friendship. By this I mean a mutual respect for and enjoyment of each other's company."

–John Gottman

Phase One of a Partnership Marriage

There are many names in the marriage literature for the first period of a couple's new relationship, which include passion stage, honeymoon stage, enchantment and romantic love. This first phase is where a couple meets, gets to know one another and falls in love. Harrar and DeMaria (2007) suggest that the focus of this initial time in a couple's relationship is enjoying their attraction to each other, creating their own world of "we," building a strong sense of trust and belonging and exploring their sexual and emotional closeness. It is a time when couples are infatuated and fall madly in love with each other.

It is during this time when a new couple shares fun and intimate activities with each other. They develop a sense of being known by their partner and create a private shared world known only to them. Inside this new world, the couple connects with each other in important ways. They share their feelings, their interests, their thoughts and their bodies with each other. They share their opinions, their judgments and their beliefs. They share their hopes and aspirations. They agree and, at times, disagree with each other. It is a time early in relationship when love is blind and the sentiment in the relationship is, "I am so happy being with you!"

Once, I was sharing with a group of couples about my second date with Martha, when we attended a community theater production of "Some Like it Hot." I shared with the group that it was on that date when Martha and I first fell in love. Martha, who was at the gathering that evening, said quite spontaneously, "No, we didn't." For a moment, I was off-balance and confused. I looked at her and said, "Well, then, what did we fall into?" She looked back at me hesitatingly and I could see she didn't quite have words for it, only that she had a sense that *something* happened that night. After a moment, she looked at me and said, "We fell into *us*." On that early date, something had been born. The way I expressed what happened between us was that we had fallen "in love." Upon reflection, we had fallen into "us."

During the birth of a couple's relationship, whether aware of it or not, each person engages in questions that are at the very heart of what is important for having a happy, healthy connection. "Do I like this person?" "Can I trust him?" "Do we trust each other?" "Can I be myself with this person?" "Is she open and honest with me?" "Do we have the same interests?" "Do we share similar values?" "Can we communicate with each other?" "Does he understand me?" "Do I feel comfortable with her?" "Do I care for this person?"

When two people meet, begin to date and develop a romantic relationship, their attraction is cognitive, emotional and physical.

For both persons, neurotransmitters are released in the brain and sexual and emotional hormones into the bloodstream that account for their intense attraction to each other. Many new couples experience being on an emotional rollercoaster. Individuals at this early phase can feel giddy and euphoric, often describing themselves as hopelessly in love. This idyllic and optimistic view of one's new relationship can last from six months to several years when those chemical reactions begin to subside.

Some of the first conversations a couple has are around what they enjoy doing, their interests, childhood memories or special hobbies. Couples also may enjoy conversing around important past experiences in their lives, where they have lived and where they have traveled or they may talk about politics, civil rights or world issues. As couples get to know each other, they may connect around their cultural backgrounds, family values and work ethics. Other couples may connect around spiritual or intellectual pursuits. These conversations weave a tapestry of common experience that results in the couple feeling that they belong together. Many couples experience that their relationship was meant to be!

As they get to know one other, a couple often spends more and more time together. This is a time when two people begin to test out being an exclusive couple. "Are we friends?" "How well do we get along?" "Do I feel at home with this person?" "Do I see a future being with this person?" "Is this relationship the real thing?" It is a time of exploration, play, discovery, intimacy, risk-taking, sharing and learning to be successful in having a mutually satisfying relationship. Being happy in the relationship, trusting each other and being free to be one's self with one's partner are all of paramount importance during this early stage of a relationship.

It is during this time that a couple makes their first important commitment to each other: *The couple invests in the possibility and promise of having a committed relationship.* Each person in the relationship asks and considers the question, "Is this person 'The One'?" "Is this relationship 'it'?" Having many conversations for connection adds depth and breadth to a new relationship and is key in the formation of an exclusive relationship where each person feels seen and heard. Being trusting, honest and loving with each other allows the couple to commit to being in a monogamous relationship. By choosing to be in the relationship in this way, the couple is able to have the freedom and the safety to take the risk to open up and to share their lives intimately with each other. They are able to create a relationship in which they both have permission to be themselves and to be free of the fear of loss or rejection. They each can accept the other person as special in their lives.

Although this stage can be a wonderful time in a couple's life together, it is by no means an easy time. Just as important as forming a safe and trusting connection with each other is learning to restore that connection when it is broken or lost. Conflict, disagreements and arguments are normal and natural in the lives of two people coming together in a new relationship. These kinds of difficult interactions break connection and harmony in relationship. Without effective tools or the conversational skills to foster their connection when it is lost, a couple runs the risk of having their new relationship fail. With tools to restore connection, couples can trust themselves to move forward with future plans that may include eventual marriage. Misunderstanding about what each person needs, different expectations around what each person wants and different cultural or religious views can challenge two people's longer-term commitment to each other. Couples can fall into patterns of interaction that can doom their relationship. Repeated broken commitments or difficulties in understanding each other's needs, wants and feelings can leave each person feeling alone, disconnected and questioning their commitment to the relationship.

For their new relationship to take hold, to root and to set a strong foundation for marriage later on, a couple must master a number of conversations in this early stage. Couples might not be thinking about having a long-term relationship, but they are having conversations for sharing a special, private and trusting relationship. They are learning what they can count on from each other and what they can expect. Such conversations allow the couple to create the frame for their relationship, called "We are a committed couple."

If a couple does not have the important conversations for what connects them, for what they are committed to and for what they value in a loving, exclusive relationship, they risk not adequately forming a sound foundation for an enduring, fulfilling partnership later on. Couples who do not engage in these formulating conversations may inadvertently sow the seeds for an unsuccessful and unsatisfying relationship. The potential pain that many couples live with and settle for in their relationship as time goes by will likely be a function of a loss of connection, a lack of clarity around their promises and commitments to each other and, ultimately, a breakdown in the container of being a "loving couple."

Important conversational tools at this stage include listening to, understanding and validating each other's feelings, needs, wants and points of view. Each person in the relationship will begin to assert their preferences, their ideas and their perspectives about how to have their relationship work. Each individual may struggle with differences in what each person wants for the relationship. A couple must talk about what is important to them and what they care about, how they will treat each other, and what is allowed and not allowed. Conversations around what they are committed to emotionally and sexually are critical. These conversations help to shape their unique sense of "couple-ness." Once a couple clarifies what they are committed to, honoring these commitments with each other creates a trusting, respectful and secure bond. The couple can invest in the promise of being a committed couple. This investment comes to fruition when the couple has built a solid foundation for their relationship through connection and commitment and the groundwork necessary for the next phase of their lives: marriage and beyond.

Central Conversations in Phase One

If you are in this phase of a new relationship, there are conversations that you can have to nurture your new friendship, explore what kinds of activities you enjoy together and deepen your understanding of each other. Other important conversational skills for you to learn at this phase are to embrace each other's feelings, communicate your needs and wants clearly, share what makes your relationship special, talk about what you are committed to and express what you appreciate about each other.

Nurturing Your Friendship. To build a loving foundation for your relationship, it is important to have conversations that allow you to connect with each other in caring, trusting and playful ways. Through learning to listen to each other, you will be able to have conversations in which you will get to know each other's interests, hopes, dreams, values and preferences as well as each other's dislikes, beliefs, attitudes and, even, prejudices. You will be able to explore what you each care about and find important in your relationship. Finally, you will learn to share and support each other in creating the kind of relationship you want together.

The core of a successful relationship (and, later on, marriage) is friendship. A friend is someone who you know, you like and you trust. In the derivation of friend, "frēond," the Old English word for friend, is the present participle of the verb frēon, "to love." A friend is someone who knows you, trusts you, likes you and with whom you feel safe to share yourself. A friend, then, literally is a person you love.

Most importantly, a friend is someone with whom you feel that you can be yourself. In a friendship, you can trust yourself. You can risk yourself and be open and honest. When two lovers are getting to know each other and become friends, they are creating a relationship in which it is safe for them to connect with each other intellectually, emotionally and physically. Trust, respect and honesty are very important ingredients in this early stage of relationship. Creating your relationship as mutually satisfying to each other and as a safe container in which you can both feel valued and appreciated builds a stable basis for your new friendship.

Playing Together. When couples are first getting to know each other and becoming friends, they participate in activities in which they have fun and enjoy being together. Playful activities can include recreational activities, such as dining out, going to movies, sightseeing or going to sporting events and leisure activities, such as reading, watching television, playing games or putting puzzles together. When couples talk about and find activities they enjoy together, they share common interests and feel a greater connection with each other. The importance of this kind of conversation for the vitality of a friendship and, ultimately, for a long-term relationship cannot be overstated.

Playfulness is what often attracts a couple to each other in the beginning of their relationship and it is often that quality to which the couple returns throughout their lives together. After thirty-nine years, Martha and I still enjoy having conversations about what we like to do and making plans to play together. Since our first dates, we've enjoyed going out to dinner, going to a movie or going to a play at a community theater. Over the years, we have also enjoyed skiing, sightseeing locally, camping across the United States and traveling overseas. While I love going into antique shops, Martha doesn't. Martha loves going to museums, which I find, at times, to be tedious. We have learned to accept our differences in interests and preferences, but have continued to share many enjoyable and playful activities over the years.

Synonyms for play are amusement, recreation, pleasure, merrymaking, romp, jest, frolic, elbowroom and leeway. When you are at play with each other, you experience freedom to be yourself, to be self-expressed and to be creative. Play in your relationship allows for curiosity, experimentation, exploration, risk-taking, humor, laughter and love. You feel safe with each other. You will find that you don't have to take life so seriously, you can laugh at yourselves and you can contribute to each other freely.

Over a lifetime, play is an important context to nurture in your relationship. Ultimately, couples in a long-term partnership marriage enjoy being with each other. They set aside time to talk, to share with each other and to engage each other in their lives. They also have ample time to be away from one another. They are in a continual dance of enjoying each other's company and of having the leeway to enjoy their own individual pursuits.

While your daily experience is not always playful, by being committed to playfulness in your relationship, you can always return to your sense of humor, to the magic of your relationship and to your love for each other. Play brings fun, frolic and pleasure into life's daily moments. When you both have the freedom to be yourselves in your relationship, at any moment, you can shift your experience of being together from significance to laughter, from difficulty to freedom and from challenge to joy.

Understanding Each Other. Being able to listen to each other is fundamental to a loving relationship. Understanding what your partner says to you is one of the most magnificent gifts you can give to them. The essence of listening is empathetic understanding. Nichols (1995) writes that it is through listening that a person "bears witness" to another person's self-expression. Bearing witness implies the act of acknowledging their humanity and their contribution to you. In fact, listening is a much more powerful act than speaking. Listening to your partner grants them their speaking, their self-expression and their very "being-ness." Your partner will feel enlivened when you listen to them. They will feel validated, seen and acknowledged when you listen and understand what they say. Through listening, you communicate to your partner that, "I see you and I hear you. I am present and attentive to your self-expression and I value what you are saying."

Each of you in your committed relationship has your own unique perspective, your own view of the world. Listening occurs when you give up your attachment to your own point of view and start to understand the world of your partner (Nichols, 1995). For effective communication to take place, each of you must attend to and grant validity to your partner's viewpoint and seek to understand what they are saying. As you understand each other, you both will feel greater connectedness. By validating each other's point of view and by giving and receiving feedback around having understood each other, you give each other a powerful gift: the gift of understanding.

Honoring, listening to and appreciating each other's point of view is key to a satisfying relationship. This can be, however, a difficult proposition at times. If you have communication difficulties, the problem may lie in the fact that you are not taking care to validate your partner's perspective, you both may be attached to your own point of view, thereby not hearing your partner's viewpoint, or you may be disregarding each other's views all together. Without fully acknowledging and taking into consideration each other's distinct perspective, you and your partner will struggle with effective and satisfying communication, which can lead to repeated frustration and upset.

When you are able to fully embrace and validate each other's points of view in a conversation, you will be able to see and understand aspects of each other's lives that may be outside your own view. A brief story will illustrate this point dramatically. A man and a woman, who are walking together in the woods on a summer's evening, stop to get a drink of water by a brook. They turn to look at each other, whereupon the woman sees a large black bear standing right behind her partner, outside of his view. The man looks at the woman and sees a hunter with a rifle pointed at the back of her head. Her partner says to her, "There's a man with a gun pointed at the back of your head!" and the woman says to her lover, "There's a black bear right behind you!" Simultaneously, they duck, the hunter pulls the trigger and the bear drops to the ground. If the couple had neglected to validate each other's point of view, disagreed with each other about what they each saw or disregarded each other's viewpoint altogether, one can only imagine the outcome. Someone might have been mauled by the bear or have been shot by the hunter.

This couple's capacity to extricate themselves from their difficult set of circumstances and to act effectively was directly related to their ability to understand the unique perspective of their partner in relationship to their own. To be effective, each person had to act on what the other person saw in coordination with what they perceived themselves. Their individual perspectives were not the same; they each needed their point of view to be heard, to be understood and to be considered valid by their partner. By including *both points of view* in the equation, however, the couple was able to understand their present circumstances in the larger context. With such understanding, the couple was able to take action that supported their relationship.

To elaborate on this point further, I'm reminded of many conversations I've heard couples have where one person is making the case for taking an action based on their view of the circumstances while their partner makes the case of another action based on the way they see their circumstances. "We've got to make more money." "No. We must lower our expenses." Or, "We should exercise more often." "I think we should eat more nutritious foods."

In such conversations, if a couple understands and considers both points of view, they not only share a common commitment, but also expand their view of what's possible. "Let's cut expenses and make more money" or "Let's eat better and exercise regularly."

In a relationship, there are, in fact, three kinds of listening with which each of you may engage. The first kind of listening is having your attention on your own personal, inner world. Let's call this "listening to your inner voice." It is this inner voice that makes judgments, has opinions and evaluates everything. When you are listening to your inner voice, you are focused on and listening to your personal concerns and worries, to what you have to do and by when, to your opinions, judgments and self-limiting beliefs, and to inner pronouncements, such as, "I can't," "I should," "I've got to" or "I don't want to." Your attention is on yourself and not significantly on anyone else or on your relationship with others.

Your inner voice says things to you all the time. Listening to your personal world consumes much of your time and your attention during each day. This is perfectly normal and natural. By listening to your inner voice, you also attune to what you feel, what you need, what you desire, what you care about, what you hope for and what you plan to do. Your inner voice will tell you what you need to pay attention to and take care of. When listening to your personal world, you bear witness to and give validity to your own experience.

The second kind of listening is listening to the world of another or to your partner that requires you to take your attention off yourself. Let's call this "listening to your partner." In a successful, loving relationship, each person becomes attuned to the needs, the feelings, the views and the hopes of their partner. Each person is interested in how the other person is doing, what they care about and what is going on in their lives. When you intently listen to your partner, you show interest in how he or she is feeling, how their day went, how their work is going or what's on their agenda. You become aware of their overall mood and, even, what they might not be saying. Listening to the world of your partner is listening for what matters to them.

The third type of listening is "listening to your relationship" or your experience of "us." When you are listening in this way, you are attuned to the health and well-being of your relationship. This third kind of listening is more of a global listening for the *quality* of your relationship (Whitworth, Kimsey-House, & Sandahl, 1998). How connected are the two of you? What is connecting the two of you at this moment? What is your experience of "us" in the present moment? What is not being said in your relationship? What is the mood of your relationship? Is connection and commitment present in your relationship or is there a sense of disconnection, separateness or distance? Are joy and love being expressed? Is there a sense of possibility and hopefulness present in your relationship or is there a sense of resignation and hopelessness? Creating and maintaining a caring and loving relationship requires an investment in time and energy. Whenever you listen for the quality of your relationship and invest in what's important to you both, you gain access to a deeper and more meaningful connection with each other.

By distinguishing these three kinds of listening, you can become aware of where you have your attention and can choose to focus your awareness for maximum impact in your relationship. Unfortunately, many people take listening for granted and simply assume that other people will listen to them and hear what they are saying. When you speak to someone else, you want that person to be listening to you; you want their attention. It is a rude awakening when you discover that, as you are speaking to your partner about an important matter, they are busy listening to their own inner voice. You can take on being responsible for making sure your partner is able to give you their attention and listen to you when you are speaking. Let them know you'd like to have a conversation about something. Ask them if they have the time to give you their attention and listen to you. If they can't speak to you at that very moment, ask them if they can let you know when they'd be able to. In same vein, when your partner wants to have a conversation with you, if the time is right, turn down the volume on your inner voice, give them your full attention and listen to what your partner wants to say to you!

Embracing Feelings. In this first phase of relationship, many couples experience a high level of satisfaction and low stress, because they've not yet made a longer-term commitment to each other and they don't typically deal with significant life issues or decisions together (Stanley & Markham, 1992). However, in a five-year longitudinal study, Markham (1981) found that one of the best predictors of long-term marital success or failure was how well a couple communicates with each other *prior* to getting married and before having significant problems in their relationship! In other words, in this early phase of your relationship, if you are able to communicate well with each other, you will have greater success in dealing with any eventual distress in your relationship and have an advantage if you choose to get married. Couples who learn to communicate well in this early phase have a better prognosis for future marital success than couples who don't (Markham, 1981).

One important lesson to learn early in a new friendship is that feelings and emotions are a natural and normal part of any human relationship. Feelings seem to come and go. It is easy to label some feelings as "good" and some feelings as "bad." It is true that some feelings, such as anger, fear and embarrassment, can be difficult to experience, but that does not make them "bad" feelings or even negative feelings. They are simply feelings. When you can learn to embrace what you are feeling, you may notice that the feeling you are having will dissipate and even disappear.

My good friend Jack, a psychologist, taught me this when I was studying in my graduate program. I was upset and angry for having taken on too many commitments and afraid that I wasn't going to be prepared for a lecture I was scheduled to give. I felt paralyzed in taking action so I called Jack. I wanted to tell him the whole story about how I had too much work to do and how I had to cancel my speaking engagement. As I began to tell him my story, he did something extraordinary; he asked me, "What are you feeling?" I said, "I am angry. I am afraid I won't be prepared for the lecture." He said, "Okay. Is it okay to feel those feelings?" I said, "No!" He said, "Okay. Is it okay not to want to have those feelings?" A bit cautiously, I said, "Yes, it is." At that moment, something amazing happened. My feelings of anger and fear started to disappear. What I saw was that I was not allowing myself to embrace the feelings I was having. I didn't want to be experiencing anger and fear. Jack had given me a way to accept what I was feeling; that it was okay not to want to feel what I was feeling. Rather than the feelings having me, I was able to have the feelings I was feeling. I was able to focus on my current situation and figure out a better course of action. I was no longer paralyzed by what I was feeling.

What I realized later was that I was able to embrace not only what I was feeling, but also how I was being about my feelings. Jack didn't ask why I was feeling what I was feeling. He didn't tell me that I shouldn't be feeling those feelings. He didn't give me advice about how I should feel or what I should do. He allowed me to identify what I was feeling and see that I was not allowing myself to have those feelings.

In early years of our relationship, Martha and I learned to help each other to identify and accept our feelings, whatever they were. We didn't tell each other not to have them; we learned to be with each other and have what we were feeling. I remember coming home from work one day, distressed and angry. Martha met me at the door, recognized that I was out of sorts as I began to launch into a story about my boss, my work and everything else I could think of that was upsetting me in that moment. She didn't ask me why I felt the way I did. She asked me two questions, "What are you feeling?" and "What happened?" I said, "I'm annoyed. The meeting got moved to this Monday and I have to write a big report this weekend instead of next weekend." I was able to get right to the point. She then said, "I understand. What do you need?" As I felt heard and understood, my anger and upset disappeared and, with Martha's support, I could then look realistically about what I was going to have to do that weekend.

Learning to accept and embrace each other's feelings in your relationship is a gift you give each other. Knowing that whatever you may be feeling at any moment can dissipate and, even, disappear, if you name it, share it with your partner and allow it to be there without having to justify it gives you a powerful way to contribute to each other. Avoid asking each other "Why?" You will simply invite justification. By using "what" questions and asking "What are you feeling?" and "What happened?" you can better understand what is going on in each other's lives and what may have triggered the feelings you are having. As you embrace your feelings, they will lessen and you will be freed up to deal effectively with your circumstances.

Communicating Your Needs Effectively. Marshall Rosenberg (2005) makes similar recommendations in his work on compassionate communication. He has examined how people can be effective in communicating their needs, wants and desires with each other. He has found people who communicate effectively connect in ways that are compassionate and develop skills to reconnect with each other when that connection breaks down and is lost. When you express yourselves with honesty and empathy so that your needs, wants and desires are taken into consideration, you relate to each other in a loving way. Communicating compassionately fosters a way of talking about difficult issues and problems respectfully, with empathy and with a commitment to nurture your relationship. There are four basic components of communicating with compassion (Rosenberg, 2005).

a. Observing and suspending judgment. When you and your spouse have an issue with each other, it is important that you separate what you observe happening from any evaluation that you might have. "This is what I saw happen." The object is to take note of what is actually happening (specific actions) in a situation that is affecting your well-being. Be specific as to what happened, who did what, when it occurred and where it happened. In other words, you acknowledge what factually happened in a situation as if you are describing it in a courtroom.

Be careful not to include your own personal interpretations, judgments or assumptions about your partner's motives (Rosenberg 2005). Avoid making generalizations using of words such as always, never, whenever, seldom and frequently. Avoid making "you" statements or pronouncements about your partner. Say what happened from your point of view. An example of what you heard or saw might be: "I heard you say…." or "I observed you doing…" instead of making a judgment, such as, "You didn't seem to care at all about what I was saying."

b. Expressing the impact of your partner's specific behavior. It is also important to communicate what impact your partner's behavior or actions had on you. At times, partners are not aware of how their behavior impacts each other. Often, it can be difficult to identify and express feelings openly and honestly with each other. It can be hard to say what you feel without justifying yourself or making someone or something the reason you feel the way that you do.

When your partner understands that their behavior has a specific impact on you that they do not consciously intend to have, they may be more willing to change. When communicating the impact of your partner's behavior, describe your internal state, including your feelings and the thoughts you are having. You want to help your partner understand how you perceived their actions and behavior. It is important that you share your internal experience in relation to what you have observed. In other words, share your feelings and your thoughts without judgment, justification or story. Instead of saying, "You weren't listening to me," describe their behavior. For instance, "When I was talking, I saw you push back your chair from the dinner table and look out the window." Then, share the impact. "I felt ignored. I thought you had stopped listening to me."

c. Identifying your needs, values or desires. In addition, it is important that you identify needs that are not being met, values that are not being honored or desires that are being thwarted. You are never angry *because* of what other people say or do. The cause of your anger is located in your own thinking or in the thoughts of blame, judgment and making something wrong. What others say and do can be a stimulus, but is never the "cause" of your feelings. It is your own thought patterns that cause you to feel the way you do. How you interpret what you hear will trigger your reactions and your feelings to what your partner says or does. When you are able to accept responsibility for your feelings, you can better identify what need you have that is being unmet or what desire you have that is being thwarted. You can also be more aware of your own expectations, values and intentions. When you are able to express your needs in an open and honest way, you have a better chance of getting them met. Several basic needs include the need for autonomy, the need for connection, the need for nurturance and the need to be understood.

d. Making requests that nurture your relationship. Being responsible for what you need from each other and for what you value in your relationship requires you to be explicit in making requests of each other. When you express your feelings and identify an unmet need that is at the source of those feelings, the next step is to make a request that clearly expresses what you want from your partner.

Requests that you make to your partner without sharing your feelings and needs may seem demanding to them because they won't understand your experience or the context in which your request is being made. By sharing your feelings and needs, your partner is able to get into your world and understand why you are making the request.

Making a request in a way that is clear, specific and concrete, specifying what you want from your partner, increases the likelihood that your request will be accepted. It certainly allows your partner to have a choice in the matter and, if your partner does not accept your request, to have the opportunity to give you a counteroffer that can still meet your needs.

Separating interpretations and judgments from what actually happens in life, sharing feelings authentically, identifying needs that are not being met and being able to make requests and promises of each other are all very important basic communication tools for you and your spouse. When you are able to learn such skills to resolve issues, problems and conflicts, you have an important arsenal of tools you can use to be successful over the long term.

Becoming a Couple. When you form an exclusive relationship, you both begin to see yourselves as tethered to each other in important ways. You invest yourselves in that relationship. "Being a couple" becomes the container for your lives and begins to shape your thoughts, feelings and actions. It shapes your concerns, your worries, your hopes and your desires. You might find yourselves thinking about each other every waking moment in the first few months, and then over time, begin to take being a couple for granted.

The transformation of going from considering yourself single and unattached to becoming a couple with another person can be both an exciting and a challenging time in your life. No longer are you thinking about just you. In addition to your own life, you must pay attention to the feelings, the thoughts, the points of view and the concerns of your partner. Your own choices, commitments and actions begin to be considered inside a new view: You are now a couple.

The foundation of your committed relationship rests on a set of shared values that guide your actions together. The values you share together can be seen as intrinsic to your "couple-ness," the glue that keeps you both deeply connected. These values reflect the very heart and soul of your relationship. Some couples value their individuality and experience being in a relationship as a loss of personal freedom or a new challenge to their self-expression. Other couples value mutual understanding, validation, communication, openness, compromise and friendship. Other couples value the freedom to express different viewpoints, emotional expressiveness and passion. Still other couples value minimizing conflict, sharing common ground, harmony and autonomy. Couples who share common values can be very successful over the long term (Gottman, 1994).

Clarifying Your Commitments. The quality of a new bond of friendship between two people is strengthened though the commitments they make with each other. The commitments you make to each other allow you to create a strong container for your relationship, where you both feel safe emotionally, socially, physically and sexually. The commitments that you keep with each other determine what you care about and what each of you can expect in the relationship. Your commitments will ultimately determine the workability, durability and health of your relationship.

Commitment is central to having a happy and healthy relationship. Early in a relationship and at points all along the way, it is important to talk about what commitment means in your relationship and what you're committing to. Many couples are unaware of what commitment means to them or what commitments they are making with each other. Many commitments remain implicit and assumed, rather than explicit.

Your perspective of what commitment means to you shapes how you relate to commitment in your relationship. For instance, commitment for one person may mean a loss of freedom, hard work and having no fun. For another person, commitment means fulfillment, freedom and an expression of one's true self. For another, it may mean obligation and duty. Your perspective or view of commitment is a composite of assumptions, conclusions, beliefs and decisions you have made growing up. Your view of commitment can unknowingly and unwitting influence your experience of vitality and aliveness in your relationship.

Stanley (2005) suggests that choice is key to having a healthy and satisfying relationship. In other words, when making a commitment, you are consciously choosing, as in "I choose this commitment." When you make such a choice, you see yourself as the author of the commitment you are making. Stanley (2005) refers to this kind of commitment as dedication. Without a sense of choice, you may experience your commitment to each other as constraining or obligatory. When the two of you commit to be in an exclusive relationship, you are making a choice that precludes other partners. When you say "yes" to your relationship, you simultaneously are saying "no" to other relationships. When you each commit to "yes," you are in a committed relationship. You are now a couple.

Appreciating Each Other. Lynn Twist (2003) in her book, *The Soul of Money*, writes, "What you appreciate, appreciates." When you appreciate each other and what you have with each other, your relationship appreciates. It grows in value. Synonyms for appreciation are gratitude, thankfulness, recognition and acknowledgment.

You and your partner can take moments when you are together and share what you appreciate or value in each other and in your relationship. This is a good habit to get into if you are talking about having a long-term relationship and even getting married. Share with each other what you love about your friendship. What do you appreciate about your partner? What strengths and talents do you see in your partner? What is so special about this new relationship in which you are investing?

Being appreciative of one another allows you to be fully aware of each other's gifts and the gifts of the relationship. Appreciation can be thought of as the antidote to taking each other for granted. With appreciation, you become aware of what is important to you in your relationship and of being grateful for what you have in your relationship. Appreciation strengthens the durability and illuminates the magnificence of your friendship. Appreciation acknowledges and reveals the quality, the brilliance and the essence of your unique relationship.

Conversations for Connection, Commitment and Being a Couple

Below I have given you a couple of conversations you can have to nurture your blossoming friendship. These conversations support you in keeping your connection alive with each other and in celebrating your unique relationship! You can find additional tools and exercises by visiting www.thepartnershipmarriagebook.com/tools and by typing in the access code "youandme" (no quotes, all lower case) to download The Partnership Marriage Phase One Toolkit to your computer.

1. Sharing What You Appreciate about Each Other. In this exercise, you each will take turns giving and receiving appreciation. Find a time and a place to be together. Sit next to each other on a couch or across from each other in chairs and get into a comfortable position. Relax and let go of everything that has been going on in your life during the day.

Be with each other without speaking for a minute or two. Taking turns, share with each other what you appreciate about each other. You can begin each sentence in different ways using the phrases below:

- What I love about you is...
- What I appreciate about you is...
- What I recognize in you is...
- What I acknowledge you for is...
- What I value in you is...
- What I enjoy about being with you is...
- What I am proud about you is...
- What you have contributed to me is...
- What I admire about you is...
- What I thank you for is...

72

2. Sharing What You Appreciate about your Relationship. Next, take turns sharing with each other what you appreciate about your relationship using the following phrases.

- What I appreciate about our relationship is...
- What I am grateful for in my relationship with you is....
- What I value about our relationship is...
- What I enjoy about our relationship is...
- What I am proud about our relationship is...
- What our relationship has contributed to my life is...
- What I admire about our relationship is...
- What I acknowledge about our relationship is...
- What I am thankful for in our relationship is...

Now, take a moment and have a conversation with each other around the following question: What is present in your experience of your relationship after engaging in this conversation?

3. Inquiring into What Commitment Means to You. In the next exercise, you will have the opportunity to inquire into your perspectives of what commitment means in your relationship. Find a comfortable place to sit together and have a conversation using the following questions to help frame your conversation:

- When you hear the word commitment, what comes to mind for you?
- What is your perspective on commitment?
- What does commitment mean in the context of a "committed" relationship?
- What does commitment mean in the context of a marriage?
- What does being committed mean to you in your relationship today?

- What does being committed mean to you in a relationship that is a true partnership?

Using a pad of paper, capture what you each are expressing. What does commitment mean to each of you? It can be a very insightful discussion. Share back and forth about your views on commitment and the role it plays in a healthy relationship, partnership and marriage.

4. Exploring the Origins of Your Ideas about Commitment. Next, explore when and where you might have learned your notions of commitment. From whom did you learn about commitment in relationship? What influences in your lives have shaped your beliefs and views about commitment in relationship? Some examples might be:

- What did your parents teach you about commitment in a relationship?
- What did other important family members teach you about commitment?
- What have your friends taught you about commitment?
- What has the media taught you?
- What have you read in books?
- What have athletes, celebrities, politicians and other famous people taught you about commitment?
- What have religious figures taught you?
- What has life taught you about commitment in relationship?

The following questions can assist you in having a very rich and robust conversation about what commitment already means to you.

- What is your understanding of commitment?
- What difference does commitment make in your relationship?
- How do you sustain commitment in your relationship?
- When commitment wanes, how do you restore your commitment?

5. Clarifying Your Commitments. Next, have a conversation to examine specific commitments in your relationship. Consider the following questions. Make notes in a notebook or on a piece of paper.

- What commitment(s) are you making (or have you made) to your partner?
- What are you not committing to (or have you not committed to) with your partner?
- What commitments are you now making in your relationship?
- What commitments are you now not making in your relationship?

After considering the following questions, take turns sharing the commitments you have written down in your notebooks. Share back and forth as you clarify the commitments in your relationship. Being explicit about your commitments is a very powerful way for two people to be in relationship together.

Chapter

5

WE'RE COMMITTED

CONVERSATIONS FOR TEAMWORK, WORKABILITY AND HAPPINESS

"Marrying is easy, it's housework that's hard."

–Proverb

Phase Two of a Partnership Marriage

This second phase begins when the couple takes the plunge to either get engaged or move into a home together (or both) and often extends into the first few years of marriage. It is a time when the couple and those around them recognize that the couple has made a significant commitment to being together in life. The focus of this second stage is for the couple to be effective in communicating and listening to each other, to set boundaries that support their relationship, to find time to nurture their experience of "us" and to learn to operate as a team around their roles and responsibilities of living together (Harrar and DeMaria, 2007). In this phase, however, the couple often comes to grips with reality, copes with disillusionment and disappointment and makes many compromises.

In this phase, a couple invests in their relationship by making the commitment to marry and be together over a lifetime. When getting engaged, a couple states publicly their promise to each other and their intention to get married at some time in the future. *It is in this phase that being together in a committed relationship transforms into the promise of getting married.* The couple resolves the question, "Is this person the one with whom I want to spend my life?" There is often much joy and happiness at this time in a young relationship.

For the couple and their families, there is a positive affirmation of love, commitment and much hope for the future. Families who were on the sidelines witnessing the birthing of the couple's relationship now begin to plan for the prospect of joining together to celebrate the marriage of their loved ones. Wedding arrangements are discussed, financial commitments are made and wedding guests are invited. As both individuals and their families participate in the wedding preparations, the couple must learn to work together in new ways to balance their own needs with those of their family members. This is often a new frontier for a couple. It can be a wonderful, yet challenging, testing ground for the couple's commitment to each other. Not only are they planning the ceremony and celebration of their public commitment to each other, but they are also learning to navigate through the expectations and the desires of extended family members; people who plan to be in their lives for many years.

It is in this second phase of a partnership marriage that a couple actually gets married. They say their marriage vows in a public gathering before a minister, priest, rabbi or justice of the peace and before a community of friends and family who themselves give their promise to support the success of the marriage. Each person says vows to love and be committed to one other in their marriage and in their life together. Their marriage is brought into existence when the person officiating the marriage ceremony says,

"By virtue of the power vested in me by the State of _____, I now declare you husband and wife." *This declaration is an act of creation that has the promise of lifelong marriage become real for the couple.*

The first months and even years of marriage can be a period of wonderment and excitement. Living together as spouses is a whole new world that the couple may have anticipated and planned for a long time. They are now "on the playing field" together. A newly married couple must learn to work out their marital roles, their household responsibilities, and the balancing of individual needs with the needs of their relationship. They are learning to communicate, problem solve, negotiate and plan together and include everything that is occurring in their lives inside the context of their marriage. In short, the couple is learning to be a team.

This second phase of marriage is a time of laying the groundwork for understanding and accepting each other on this new playing field (Harrar and DeMaria, 2007). It is a time when the couple gets to know what living with their loved one is *really* like, day in and day out. Each person now is a witness to their partner's behavioral patterns and habits that they may or may not have seen or known before. Couples in this second phase begin to see each other as having different interests, preferences, attitudes, opinions and beliefs. They discover that they do things differently. They find out that they each do the laundry or wash the dishes or organize their dresser drawers in different ways. What their partner likes to eat, how they like to spend their free time or what they like to watch on television may be in sharp contrast to what they had expected going into marriage. Personal differences begin to emerge, expectations are challenged and disappointments burst those ideal images each person has about "the way it is supposed to be." It is a time when reality sets in and the sentiment in the relationship may turn to, "What was I thinking?"

When Martha and I got married in 1974 at the height of the women's movement, many feminist leaders were espousing equal rights for women at home and in the workplace. These ideas influenced our relationship. We recognized that our marriage was not going to look like the ones our parents had when we were growing up in the 1950s. At first, we experienced confusion, bewilderment and ineffectiveness in our roles and conflict over who was going to do what. We knew, however, times were changing, we loved each other and we wanted things to work.

When we moved to Hartford, Connecticut in 1977, I started graduate school at The University of Connecticut and Martha got a job working as a budget analyst for the City of Hartford. We were not consistently getting the household chores done in our five-room apartment. We had no clear system of agreements around our roles and responsibilities, and this led to bickering and arguments. Finally, we both knew we had to talk this out. When we actually started talking, we found we were equally frustrated and judgmental about what was <u>not</u> getting done and <u>who</u> was not doing it! We were both thinking: "What is he/she expecting of me? That's his/her job! Why isn't he/she just getting it done?"

In our first attempt to clarify who was going to do what, we struggled but we managed to come up with a system of negotiating all of our household responsibilities. We were committed to equality and fairness to which we added the essential ingredient of choice. Without the experience of having choice in the matter, nothing was going to work to sustain a sense of partnership. With choice in the equation, our conversation around daily chores led to teamwork, workability and effectiveness in managing these unrelenting household activities over time. In fact, we have returned to the task of negotiating household activities many times over our thirty-nine years of marriage. When we had children, when our jobs changed, when we moved overseas and when other extenuating circumstances arose, we usually needed to renegotiate our responsibilities at home. This one accomplishment made a huge difference in our marriage!

Many couples go into marriage with a vision of starting a family, buying a house and having successful careers. At this time in our lives, Martha and I were putting off the thought of having children or owning a home. We had enough on our plates with Martha starting her career and me in graduate school. Michelle Weiner-Davis (2001) writes that is it ironic that, at this stage, when couples begin to feel at odds with each other, they are also often making large, life-altering decisions, such as having children, starting a career or going to graduate school. It is at this time, when teamwork is so critically required, that couples must learn how to have many important conversations. In the second phase of marriage, couples must focus their conversations on whether they are working as a team or not, how well their commitments and arrangements with each other are working and what kind of life they are building together.

Couples who fail to be successful at such conversations may experience many arguments and disagreements or an avoidance of conflict and a pretending that everything is just fine when it's not. They may run the risk of being ineffective at taking care of basic responsibilities and meeting each other's needs and wants. They may be unsatisfied in their marriage. The view of themselves and their marriage as being happy and successful in the future can begin to erode and be thrown into doubt. Couples who have workable agreements in their relationship, take care to meet each other's needs and learn to work as a team nurture the long-term health and vitality of their marriage.

At this early phase, a couple can explore their notions and ideas of what constitutes a happy or sound marriage, discuss what they want in their marriage and design their commitments with each other. They'll have to figure out what works and what doesn't work for them in a whole host of areas, such as money, sex, recreation or time with friends and family. Just in the act of living together and being committed to having their marriage work they may find they have to give up ideas about the way they thought it was going to be in their marriage. They now find themselves on the court of life together and they discover it's up to them to make their marriage work.

How will they work together as a team? How will they design their roles and responsibilities so that each of them is satisfied? How will they respect and manage their personal space and privacy to ensure a trusting and workable relationship? How will they honor what is important to their relationship at the same time attend to their relationships with family and friends? How will they balance the commitments they have to themselves and to each other with all the commitments they have with work, with friends and with other community or professional groups. Boundaries will need to be set so that the marital relationship can be a safe and trusting space for the couple. Couples will need time for themselves. Time to play. Time to relax. Time to get away. Time to be intimate. The connection the couple has with each other will need to be nourished and cared for, as their responsibilities of a shared life together become a more pressing reality.

Central Conversations in Phase Two

During this time in your relationship there are important conversations that you and your partner can have to explore your notions of marriage and the kind of marriage that you want together, to figure out what is going to work for you now that you have committed to a future together and to work out your roles and responsibilities. Also, there are conversations in which you can clarify important boundaries for your relationship and plan times to enjoy each other. At this phase, it is important that you have conversations to foster teamwork, bring workability into your day-to-day lives and begin to create the shared life that you desire.

Exploring Ideas and Notions of Marriage. People have all kinds of ideas and notions about marriage. Growing up, we form our ideas about marriage by watching how our own parents navigated their marital landscape. We form beliefs and judgments about marriage by what we watch on the television or at the movie theater, by what we read in newspapers and magazines and by witnessing the success or failure of the marriages of our friends and family members. We adopt different beliefs about what marriage is and what it can be. Sometimes, we think that marriage is a one-size-fits-all kind of phenomena when, in truth, every marriage is distinct, one of a kind.

One of the most prevalent beliefs is that marriage will make you happy. There is good evidence, in fact, that people who get married and stay married are happier than single or divorced individuals (Waite & Gallagher, 2000). But does marriage make you happy? On the surface, it is a prevalent belief that seems to be true. You have to stop and think, though, that with the very high divorce rate in this country, marriage, in and of itself, will not "make" a couple happy. I may think my marriage or my partner will make me happy, but deep down, I know that isn't quite how it works. I must bring my happiness to my marriage.

Scott Stanley (2005) suggests that it is a good idea that couples talk about the kind of marriage they want to have together prior to getting married. In fact, he advocates that married couples should regularly discuss their vision of their marriage. If you are like many young married couples, you won't discuss your beliefs or ideas about marriage until after your wedding day. Once you're married, you may find out you have very different ideas about how your marriage should work. People may have told you that marriage is really hard work, but you have no idea what that actually means. As newlyweds, you may think that a good marriage is one that doesn't have any problems or one in which there are no arguments or conflict. In other words, a good marriage is problem-free. Some common beliefs that I have heard couples say about marriage are "You will live happily ever after," or "Love will make marriage work," or "Marriage is for soul mates." While these beliefs have some value and validity, you may find that marriage doesn't quite work out that way.

If you are in a committed relationship and are reluctant or ambivalent about getting married, you also have your own views on marriage. You may feel that marriage doesn't fundamentally work, it is broken, it is toxic or it is a trap. If you are cohabitating with your partner, you may feel that marriage will spoil a perfectly good relationship so why get married. You might think that you can go into marriage with the idea that if it doesn't work, you can simply get out of the marriage by getting a divorce. With all of these beliefs, ideas and judgments about marriage swirling around, often unexamined, it is a good idea to spend time with your partner having conversations (more than one) about what marriage means to you both and what you want in your marriage.

Designing Your Marriage. Over the course of your marriage, you will make commitments to each other, creating who you are for each other and for your relationship. Through making such declarative statements to each other, you have a shared stake in the quality of your relationship and the kind of marriage you are going to create. Here are examples of such commitments you can make to each other:

- I love you; we love each other
- I trust you; we trust each other
- I am your friend; we are friends
- I respect you; we respect each other

- I promise to be faithful to you; we promise to be faithful to each other
- I hold you as an equal; we are equals in our relationship

Such declarations shape the experience of each of you has in your relationship. Let's look at the declaration, "I love you." Many people experience love primarily as a feeling. If they have the feeling of love, then they must be "in love." They know they love their spouse because they feel love. If they do not feel love, then they may be unsure whether they actually love the other person. There are other people who understand love as a concept or an idea they got from reading a book or seeing a movie. Such a concept becomes an idealized state to attain. They will know they are in love when the circumstances of their life match that idealized concept of love.

Still many other couples know they love each other even when neither one of them are experiencing love or when their lives do not fit neatly into any idealized picture of a loving relationship. They know that they love each other even when they get mad at each other. They love each other when they are apart for long periods of time, when their jobs take too much of their attention, when they are in conflict about something or when money is tight and they can't give each other what they want.

Love for such a couple is declared. They love each other because they say so. Having given their word to each other allows them to know they love each other even when they may not experience the feeling of love. All the circumstances of life, including working hard, having little time for each other, arguing about something or feeling out of communication with each other are held in a context of love. At every moment, you can know that you love each other regardless of the circumstances of your life.

There are three commitments that both of you can make in your marriage that help you to create a healthy and vibrant relationship. These commitments are having your relationship work for *both* of you, being 100% responsible for the quality of your relationship and making the well-being of your marriage the *top priority* for each of you.

Creating a Context of You and Me. A successful and healthy relationship by its very nature requires a context of you <u>and</u> me. The context of "you and me" provides a powerful perspective for you and your partner where you know that, for your relationship to be successful, it must be a "win-win" proposition for you both. Each of you must satisfactorily attend to each other's individual needs, desires and goals as well as those of your relationship. You each must be committed to having the relationship work for both of you, individually as well as collectively.

It is difficult to have a satisfying or sustainable relationship if one of you in the relationship feels that what is going on in the relationship is not working. If the relationship is not working for you, it cannot work for your partner. The perspective "win-lose" in relationship does not and cannot work to support the long-term viability of your marriage; it is, in fact, an illusion. In your relationship and in your marriage, you both are either winning (win-win) or you are losing (lose-lose). To have things work in a relationship, you must commit yourselves to a fundamental truth: "For our relationship to work for each of us, it must work for both of us *and*, for it to work for both of us, it must work for each of us."

Creating a 100% - 100% Model of Responsibility for Your Marriage. Many couples early in their marriage set up a model of responsibility that might be called 50% - 50%. If each person in the relationship does their 50%, then all 100% of what needs to be done gets accomplished and presumably both persons will be happy and satisfied. While this model appears to have its merits, it is insufficient to creating a workable relationship. If you have this kind of arrangement, as soon as you do not keep your bargain to do your 50% in the relationship, your partner may experience resentment, frustration and a sense of being taken advantage of. You may feel the same way when your partner doesn't keep their 50% of the bargain. It is a model that is based on what each person is <u>doing in</u> a relationship, rather than based on who each person is <u>being for</u> the relationship.

A committed relationship requires a model of 100% - 100% responsibility. Responsibility in this framework is the act of owning your own happiness and creating your responsibility for it by saying: "I am completely responsible for my happiness. And while I am not ultimately responsible for my partner's happiness, I am committed to it." In other words, if I am not happy about something in my life, I will speak up. If I see that my partner is not happy about something, I will speak up and find out what's bothering them. This clear understanding of responsibility, together with a commitment to each other's happiness, is an important aspect of workability in a relationship.

If both of you are responsible for your own happiness and committed to the happiness of each other, then who is ultimately responsible for the workability of your relationship? Both of you are. In other words, if there is something that is not working in my relationship with Martha, I will speak up. And so will she. In your relationship, both of you can naturally commit yourselves to being 100% responsible for the workability and happiness in your marriage.

Having the Quality of your Marriage Be Your Top Priority. We live in a world where we are focused on our individual lives, oriented to our work, bombarded by the media and driven to meet insatiable material needs. This leaves many of us less connected, less intimate and less focused on the quality of our marriage. Here is what may happen in your marriage as a result:

- You are too busy to put a priority on your marriage

- You get too focused on your children or your individual work lives
- You take your partner for granted
- You watch too much television or spend too much time on the Internet
- You stop dating or creating time for your relationship
- You don't spend enough time with friends and family
- You disagree about how much work to put into your marriage

Does this sound familiar? Here's another perspective. Adopt the idea that the quality of your marriage is your #1 priority. Imagine what your life would look like if you made the quality of your relationship and the well-being of your marriage your top priority for the rest of your lives. Consider the following questions:

- What becomes possible in your marriage?
- What do you see about the quality of your lives together over the long haul?
- Where would you both put your attention?
- What would you contribute to your children?
- How would you go about solving problems in your relationship?
- How would you work together to realize not only your individual dreams but also your joint dreams?
- What would the quality of your friendships be like in your lives?

Just for a little contrast, imagine that you both do *not* make the quality of your marriage your #1 priority. Imagine that there is always something more important that displaces your commitment to the quality of your relationship. It could be your work, your parents, your children, your finances or your friends. Ask yourselves the question: "How is it going to turn out long term if something else is *always* more important than the quality of our marriage?"

Consider that the quality of your marriage is the context for everything in your life to work. Everything in your lives can occupy an important place inside the context of your commitment to each other and the quality of your marriage. In a partnership marriage, the quality of your marriage is *your* top priority.

Boundaries that Support Your Relationship. When Martha and I lived together in Lincoln, Nebraska, just prior to getting married, we had to sort out a whole host of issues, e.g., sharing a physical space together, respecting personal privacy and determining what was okay to share with family and friends about what was going on in our relationship. Growing up, Martha enjoyed keeping a diary. I knew that because she had told me that she had written about our first dates in her diary. She specifically asked me not to read her diaries. In making that request, she wanted to create a sense of safety around her personal privacy in our relationship. To this day, I have honored that commitment I made to her over forty years ago to refrain from reading her diaries or personal communications from others.

In the early days of marriage, it is important for you to set boundaries with each other regarding privacy and personal space. Having physical space in your household that you can call your own is vitally important to establish a healthy psychological space for each of you. Having your own closet and chest of drawers for your clothes, a desk or a workspace or even your half of the medicine cabinet to keep your toiletries allows you to have space for your belongings. Being able to have places in your home where you can keep your keepsakes and special private possessions, such as jewelry, diaries, books and papers, honors each of you as individuals in your marriage. Other important boundaries for you to consider are around reading each other's mail, text messages or email, being on each other's computer (if you both have one) or even where you sit at the breakfast table. Such conversations establishing healthy physical and psychological boundaries in your lives build trust and respect in your relationship.

You also need to establish healthy boundaries with your family and their friends that build trust and confidence in the integrity of your marriage. Make agreements with each other around discussing your personal or marital problems with family members and friends. When is it okay to talk about your marriage or your spouse with others without your partner's permission or your partner being present? Extended family involvement in your lives can be an area of both joy and challenge depending on whether you and your spouse discuss the nature of that involvement, what is okay to talk about with others and what's off limits. Who is going to be involved in the decisions around family visits during the holidays? When should extended family members be involved in the concerns and business of your relationship, such as money matters, health concerns, childcare or household issues? Who makes those decisions? Often, the best policy is to err on the side of mutual decision-making with your spouse.

Creating Time for "Us." Couples who put their relationship first nurture their marriage. They think about what is best for their relationship and they plan time to be together. How well are you putting your relationship first and finding time with each other? Doherty (2001) suggests that there are many areas in which couples can nurture their relationship by creating time for "us."

Find times to connect throughout the day to support the health and well-being of your committed relationship or your marriage. It is at these times when you can pay attention to each other and reinforce that your relationship with your spouse is special to you. Doherty (2001) calls these times rituals of connection. Examples of such connection rituals may include going out for coffee together, checking in with each other when you return home from work or finding times to catch up on the day's events.

There are also times in marriage when you share your love in intimate ways. Doherty (2001) calls these love rituals in which you express your affection and passion for each other. These love rituals are unique to your private relationship. Having sex is an important time for you to express love and affection. Other examples of times when you express love to each other may be going to bed at the same time and/or finding times to share personal feelings, thoughts or insights. Such self-disclosure allows you to share your intimate experiences with each other, your hopes and dreams for the future and your appreciation for one another.

Finding time to play can take a whole host of forms, from dining out, shopping or going to a community fair to playing tennis together, spending the day sightseeing or hiking in the woods. The purpose of playtime is quite simply for you to have fun and enjoy being together. In addition, relaxation and quiet times are times when you enjoy each other's company at home. You may take pleasure in activities such as putting together a puzzle, playing a board game or watching a DVD, or in more solitary activities such as reading or playing games on your tablets while sitting by a fire in the fireplace. Also, by celebrating special occasions in your lives, you honor those memorable moments that are uniquely yours. Such times include your wedding anniversary, your birthdays, Valentine's Day, the day you met or got engaged and other important dates that hold special significance for the two of you.

The purpose of dating is to go out in the evening or on a weekend afternoon, just the two of you, to connect emotionally through conversation and pleasurable activities. Dating includes going out to dinner, going to a movie, concert or play, attending a sporting event or taking a drive into the countryside. You can also nurture your relationship by getting away for the weekend for rest and relaxation, for more rigorous activity or for fun and exploration. Such weekends away might involve staying in a Bed and Breakfast, going skiing or golfing, sightseeing in a big city or camping in the mountains. Lastly, you can renew your relationship by getting away for longer periods of time on vacation. Vacations can include traveling abroad or to unexplored regions of the United States, taking a cruise into the fjords of Norway, camping in a national park, renting a cabin on a lake in New Hampshire or taking a week to ski in the Rockies. When you get away from work and your daily concerns, you can use the extended time away to renew yourselves and your relationship.

Creating Workability in Your Marriage. In his systematic study of marriage, John Gottman (1994) identified factors that influence the success and failure of marriage. In particular, his research on 2000 couples found that conflict is not necessarily unhealthy, especially when it airs issues, grievances and complaints. In other words, how well a couple participates together to resolve issues, discuss problems, negotiate with each other and plan for the future is one of the best ways to diagnose the health of the relationship. Additionally, Gottman (1994) found that he could predict with 94% accuracy which couples were headed for divorce based solely on the couples' viewpoints of their marital history, their current perspectives on their marriage and their patterns of interaction with each other. Overall, the quality of a couple's skills in coping, adapting, problem solving and negotiating were found to be important in dealing with life's demands and crucial to the longevity of their committed relationship.

What seems more important than actually solving issues and resolving problems is feeling good about the interactions that you are having with each other. For you to have a contented and happy marriage, you must maintain a healthy balance of positive and negative interactions towards each other. Stable marriages exhibit a 5 to 1 ratio of positive to negative interactions.

In your marriage, if you are unable to maintain a 5 to 1 ratio of positive to negative interactions and tend toward a much higher percentage of negative interactions, you will likely have more significant problems and be heading toward trouble in your relationship. Such negative interactions may include criticism, contempt, emotional withdrawal and defensiveness. Anger can be particularly destructive if it accompanies these other behavioral patterns.

What are typical stable couples doing? They are maintaining the 5 to 1 ratio of positive to negative interactions. These couples tend to be less extreme in their feelings, less critical, less contemptuous, less defensive and more engaged in listening. Examples of positive interaction include showing interest, being affectionate, being caring, being appreciative, being concerned, being empathetic, being accepting, sharing humor and laughing together. The basic ingredients in marriage are love and respect.

Gottman (1994) suggests that in marriages that are stable, certain kinds of negativity may actually have a positive function in the marriage and be healthy for a partnership. Negativity and conflict can sometimes serve a positive function of renewal. On the other hand, too much negative or too little positive interaction in your relationship can spell disaster for your marriage. You, like all successful couples, must learn how to resolve problems and issues as they arise and how to interact successfully with each other on a daily basis. In the first years of marriage, one area where you may experience increased conflict is in establishing teamwork around negotiating and completing household tasks.

Creating Teamwork around Household Chores. It could be said that to have a successful marriage in today's society, you have to learn to negotiate everything: the household tasks, money, parenting, sex, etc. Given that most men and women today are pursuing careers and working full time, both individuals need to be involved in discussing their roles and household responsibilities.

The effectiveness of your conversations and the workability of these arrangements are critical to the quality of your lives and to giving you a pathway to creating the future you want to have together.

A significant problem for many couples, though, is that they *don't* effectively negotiate the roles and responsibilities in their marriage and fall into marital roles that were given to them by their families of origin and/or that don't work in meeting the challenges of today's demanding lifestyles. Many women still take care of the lion's share of the household tasks and childrearing activities even though they, like their husbands, are working full time. Today, the dual expectations for equality and equity in marriage require greater emphasis on negotiating household responsibilities that can foster mutual satisfaction and a sense of partnership.

When learning to live with someone else in a new marriage, one of the unrelenting, day-to-day challenges is getting all of the household tasks done to the satisfaction of both parties. You initially may attempt to work out household responsibilities within a paradigm of marital roles that you both learned from your parents or grandparents while you were growing up. You may soon discover, though, that having one of you be responsible for the bulk of the household chores while the two of you both have full-time jobs may be an unrealistic way to manage your lives.

If you don't have an effective and satisfying way to negotiate your household responsibilities, you can stumble along for quite some time, never quite feeling "on the same page." Household chores don't get done and you both may feel that you have a lack of teamwork. The lack of planning and alignment around completing household responsibilities can lead to frustration, a loss of trust, resentments and regrets, accusation and defensiveness. Patterns of interactions may develop that can last for years. With a mutual commitment to equity, equality and effectiveness, you and your partner do not have to put up with any of this.

Negotiating Household Responsibilities. If it is time for you to negotiate your household responsibilities, make agreements with each other and work as a team, it works to first discuss what is important to each of you around how you go about making your agreements with each other. Here are a number of questions to consider:

- What is important to you in terms of the negotiation process? Examples might be:
  o Suspending judgment of each other
  o Respecting each other's feelings and desires
  o Listening for what tasks each person wants to be responsible
- What is important in the agreements that you make to each other? Examples might be:
  o Having choice in the matter
  o Having agreements that are equitable
  o Following through with the commitments that you make to each other
- What is important around the eventual result and experience of teamwork? Examples might be:
  o Experiencing "win-win" in your relationship
  o Being mutually satisfied
  o Experiencing yourselves as being a team

Next, write down every household task you both can think of that has to be completed around your house. For instance, the list may include paying the bills, doing the dishes, doing the laundry, taking care of the cars, dusting, cooking, feeding the dog, etc. Put each discrete activity on one list. The list might actually be shorter than what you originally thought. Trust that you both know what needs to be done around your house to have your lives run smoothly.

After you have made the complete list of household responsibilities, talk with each other about what is involved in completing each task and what a completed task looks like for you. You may have the greatest differences of opinion in this conversation. For instance, you may wash the dishes differently than your partner. Although you recognize that your partner does things differently, you both need to be able to agree on what "clean dishes" look like. For some responsibilities, you might also need to negotiate how often some activities are to be performed at home. One of you may want the vacuuming done twice a week, while your partner is happy with the vacuuming being done only once a week. Once you have agreed on what each household task involves, take turns choosing household responsibilities.

It is important that each of you have the freedom to choose whatever you want to choose with the understanding that, if you choose an activity, it will be your responsibility to regularly complete that household task to the mutual satisfaction of both you *and* your partner. Accountability here means that you each understand that you will hold yourselves to account to your partner for completing the responsibilities you've chosen.

Start with a flip of a coin if you need to. Take turns looking at your list and choosing an activity that you will be completely responsible and accountable for. One of you begins by choosing a household task and then your partner follows by choosing one. Repeat working this way until you have chosen all activities. Toward the end of the process, you may notice that several responsibilities remain on your list that neither of you want to take on. That's okay. If that occurs, take some additional time, break down what is involved and then come up with a negotiated settlement. You may find that you can do this with relative ease. If you cannot find resolution, you can come back to the activity at a later time.

One of the things that you may also notice as you are negotiating is that you may tend to choose activities that conform to sex role stereotypes. For instance, you might find that you, as the wife, choose cooking and laundry while your spouse, as the husband, ends up choosing to take care of the lawn and the trash. The important aspect is that both of you are satisfied and happy with your agreed-upon arrangement.

It works to agree that neither of you will tell your partner how to do their household tasks as long as what gets accomplished leaves both of you satisfied. If either of you completes a household activity that results in not meeting the agreed-upon satisfaction criteria, your partner has the right to object. A very useful rule to adopt in your marriage is: Each of you has "the right to complain" *only* when the other person is not fulfilling an explicit agreement that you have previously negotiated.

You both may find that the nice part about negotiating household activities in this way is that much of your day-to-day bickering and complaining about what is not getting done clears up so long as you both honor your agreements with each other. Expectations can be clarified and you may find yourselves more satisfied with how things are going around the house. If there is a problem, you can resolve the problem much faster. Sometimes one of you may not do what you agreed to do. If your arrangement is not working, you can re-negotiate. Over time, you will find yourselves able to negotiate these activities with greater ease. Whenever one of you says you will be responsible for an activity, the other person can be fairly certain it will get done.

You both can come back to this way of negotiating household activities time and time again throughout your marriage, particularly when major events have occurred, such as the birth of children, a change of jobs or a move to a new home. This process of negotiating what needs to be done will leave you with the experience of teamwork. It will allow you to focus on other aspects of your lives (careers, family, traveling, etc.) and on what's important to you in your relationship.

Why I Never "See" the Laundry. This section could also be entitled "Why Martha Never Sees the Trash." Let me explain. One of the choices I made almost thirty-five years ago in my relationship with Martha was that I would be responsible for taking out the trash. I like to take out the trash. I do it regularly every Thursday morning, every week. When I walk into a room, I often notice how much trash there is in the wastebasket. If I notice that a wastebasket is full, I automatically empty the trash into the bigger trash basket in the kitchen. When I see that the kitchen basket is full, I tie up the plastic trash bag and I put it in the large bin outside. I do this all the time. I do it gladly.

Some time ago, however, I became curious: Why is it that Martha rarely does this activity spontaneously? In other words, why does it seem that she never "sees" the trash? Routinely, she (and my grown children when they are home) walks right past a full wastebasket and rarely empties it. Sometimes, someone in the family will attempt to put something else in an already overflowing and bursting kitchen basket. It appears that they do not even see that the basket is full or what needs to be done. Why don't they just tie it up and take it outside to the large trash container?

It occurred to me that no one else empties the trash because they don't see the trash in the same way I do. When I see a full trash basket, I am "called" into action to empty it. I see the trash because I made a commitment to emptying the trash, a choice I made many years ago. When I made that choice, I became The-Person-Who-Takes-Care-Of-The-Trash. As a result, the trash occurs for me differently than for Martha. Knowing this allowed me to let go of any resentment or irritation I have had about being the only person who takes out the trash. Martha will actually tell you that one of my favorite moments of the week is when the garbage trucks arrive to haul away the garbage that I have put on the curbside that morning!

For Martha, the analogous situation is doing the laundry. In the early stages of our marriage, Martha committed to take care of washing and drying the clothes. She has completed this task regularly and responsibly for years. In our relationship, she is The-Person-Who-Takes-Care-Of-The-Laundry. Just as Martha will help me with the trash from time to time, she will occasionally ask me to assist her with the laundry. We help each other gladly. On a regular basis, though, I never "see" the laundry in the same way that she does. I am rarely called into action to do it. I rarely see doing the laundry as something that I need to do. Why? I never chose to do it. Martha, my partner, did.

Conversations for Teamwork and Workability

Below I have provided you a couple of conversations you can have to support you in creating the kind of marriage you want together. Specifically, in these conversations, you can explore your beliefs and ideas about marriage and share about what you both see as possible if you take on having a "you and me" relationship, being 100% responsible for the quality of your relationship and making the well-being of your marriage a top priority. These conversations support you in creating effective teamwork and workability in your marriage! You can visit www.thepartnership-marriagebook.com/tools and type in the access code "youandme" (no quotes, all lower case) to download The Partnership Marriage Phase Two Toolkit to your computer.

1. Exploring your Ideas and Notions about Marriage. It can be valuable to explore your unexamined ideas and expectations about marriage with each other. Find the time to talk with each other about what you imagine a happy marriage looks like. You can have a great conversation using the following questions to open up the dialogue:

- What are your personal ideals about marriage?
- What are your personal beliefs about marriage?
- What are your personal expectations about marriage?
- What do you wish for in your marriage?

By engaging in these questions, your sharing will reveal some of your current perspectives about marriage. You both may find that you have a good solid foundation in how you think about marriage. You also may find areas where you disagree. As you share your points of view, you might also consider:

- From whom or from where did you adopt your ideals, beliefs and expectations about marriage?
- What are some of the values or attitudes in our society that have shaped your view of marriage?
- What are some of the unexamined beliefs or assumptions about marriage in our culture today?
- What are some of the myths we have about marriage in our culture?
- What do you say is the purpose of marriage?

These questions are designed to assist you and your fiancé or spouse to connect with each other around your ideas about what marriage means to you. You may discover that you have your own personal myths about marriage. You might also find that you are willing to give up some of your own time-honored notions about marriage for the sake of the kind of marriage you and your partner could create together. Your marriage is unique and distinct from anyone else's. You have an extraordinary opportunity to design the kind of marriage you want together!

2. Examining What's Possible in Taking on The Three Commitments. The three commitments that you can make to help you to create a solid and strong foundation for a healthy and vibrant marriage are having your relationship work for *both* of you, being 100% responsible for the quality of your relationship and having the well-being of your marriage the *top priority* for each of you.

Together, have a conversation around these questions:

- What is possible when you each take on a "you and me" relationship?
- What can you achieve together when you adopt a "win-win" perspective?

- What is possible when each of you commit to being 100% responsible for your own happiness?
- What is possible when you each take on a stance of being 100% - 100% responsible for the quality of your relationship?
- What is possible if you each make the well-being of your marriage a top priority?
- What shared dreams are possible for you and your spouse?
- What are you passionate and excited about?
- What might a fulfilling, lifelong marriage look like for you?

Chapter

6

INVESTING IN US

CONVERSATIONS FOR PERSONAL GROWTH, SOLVING PROBLEMS AND SUCCESS

"All married couples should learn the art of battle as they should learn the art of making love. Good battle is objective and honest—never vicious or cruel. Good battle is healthy and constructive, and brings to a marriage the principles of equal partnership."

–Ann Landers

Phase Three of a Partnership Marriage

The central conversations in the third phase of a partnership marriage turn to the personal growth and success of each individual and to that of the marriage itself. Names for this phase in the marriage literature are the rebellion stage, power struggle, the seven-year itch and the stage of self-knowledge (Harrar and DeMaria, 2007). This stage of marriage often begins in the fourth, fifth or sixth year of marriage when the couple's concerns turn to juggling all the commitments involved in raising children, managing dual careers, managing the home and socializing with friends.

Having responsible jobs, planning for the future, and having children are major focuses of the first five to seven years of marriage. In these early years, a couple must learn to work and live together while managing all these responsibilities. Many unforeseen daily stresses challenge a young couple's commitment to each other. At this third phase of marriage, a couple invests in the possibility of being successful over the long haul. Up until this time, individual hopes and dreams may have been put on the back burner for the sake of the relationship. It is a time when both individuals in the marriage are asking questions that are at the very heart of who they are and what they are committed to. They may be asking themselves, "Can I grow and develop in this marriage?" "Can I get what I really need and want?" "Can I fulfill my dreams in my marriage?" How the couple is able to meet each other's needs, support each other's goals and be authentic with each other has consequences for the long-term viability of their marriage.

In order for marriage to be successful long term, a couple at this phase must recommit to the promises they made on their wedding day. On that day, most couples say vows that express their commitment "to have and to hold for better or for worse, for richer and for poorer, in sickness and in health *and* to love and cherish… until death do us part." These vows suggest that, over the course of a lifetime, *everything* that occurs in one's life together, all the good things <u>and</u> all the bad things must ultimately be accepted and held inside the context of marriage. Children will be born and family members will die. Fortunes may be made and lost. Educational degrees will be earned, careers will be fulfilled and great accomplishments will be made. People will get sick, unexpected tragedies may occur and children will leave home. To grow, to accept each other and to be successful individually and together, both persons must learn to deal effectively with what life presents them. It is imperative that a couple recommit to the quality of their marriage in the face of any and all of life's circumstances. It is in this recommitment to the quality of their marriage that a couple is able to experience their relationship as their primary context for all of life, for better or for worse. This recommitment is also a major challenge, if not the most important challenge, of phase three of a partnership marriage.

Before couples can put all four feet fully inside their marriage, it is normal for them to re-assess and question that very commitment. It is a time when many couples face a critical fork in the road (Weiner-Davis, 2001). They must answer the question whether they can be happy and successful together and, ultimately, whether their marriage can thrive. Couples may become disillusioned with each other, unable to come to grips with different parts of each other, such as personal habits, individual interests, attitudes, idiosyncrasies, political viewpoints, prejudices, etc., that are upsetting, troublesome or unacceptable. Over time, waistlines may bulge, sex may become more infrequent, sports on television may dominate attention and disappointments with one's day-to-day experience in marriage may deepen. It is in this third phase of marriage when each person may be asking, "Is this it?" or "Is this all there is?" and the sentiment in the marriage may turn to "I'd be happier if *you'd* change."

The challenge of this phase is for the couple to support each other in moving toward their personal goals, to effectively resolve conflicts so that their relationship is nurtured, to heal past hurts, and to be truthful, honest and real with each other so that *both* individuals *and* their relationship can grow (Harrar & DeMaria, 2007). If the couple is unable meet these challenges and resolve critical issues, they each run the risk of being disconnected, feeling alone and harboring real concerns about whether their marriage is going to last. They may find themselves living in a constant state of struggle and turmoil, where they each feel they can't have what they really want unless the other person changes. Their relationship may devolve into "you or me." It is worth noting that many couples having difficulties in this phase of marriage seek professional help in the form of marital therapy.

During this time, interpersonal conflicts, financial issues, stresses at work, extended family expectations or simply managing the daily responsibilities may be overwhelming. It is natural for a couple to begin to feel trapped or stuck in their marriage, wishing that things could turn out differently. With the loss of the picture of "the way it was supposed to be," the couple often reassesses their commitment to their marriage. This questioning of one's original commitment to marriage is normal and natural. The innocence of the first period of marriage gives way to a more mature re-examination of what each person wants in the relationship. With time, the couple comes to the realization that, for their relationship to work, each partner must be happy and be able to fulfill their dreams in their marriage. There may be a shifting of marital roles, household responsibilities or mutual agreements within the marriage. A higher priority is placed on balancing the goals of each person with the teamwork necessary for mutual satisfaction.

Unfortunately, the full realization of this stage can be elusive for many couples who don't resolve the essential imperative of the third stage, which is to recommit fully to their marriage and step in "with all four feet." Couples who do not make it successfully through this third marital stage can find themselves living parallel lives with a lack of teamwork, a loss of happiness, a feeling of being alone and little shared meaning with their spouse. This state inside marriage can go on, sadly, for years, particularly, if each person gives up his or her will to have their marriage work. Couples who give up will see no possibility of long-term fulfillment or success together and have no sense of a future or of being able to have their marriage work. Their connection and commitment to each other become tenuous. This condition can lead to cynicism, resignation and despair for spouses in such a marriage unless they seek professional help.

Couples who learn to communicate compassionately, to fight fairly, to apologize for their hurtful behavior and to forgive their partner's misdeeds develop important tools for their long-term happiness and success. They learn to express what they want for themselves and their relationship so that not only both individuals "win," but also their relationship is nurtured as well. They recognize that for their marriage to be fulfilling and enduring, they must create a commitment to "you, me *and* us." The health and well-being of their relationship become a priority in which they both are able to support one another in getting their needs met, in fulfilling their goals and in caring for their relationship. These couples are able to successfully transition to the fourth stage of a partnership marriage.

After a significant investment in their marriage in the first few years, couples in phase three of a partnership marriage refocus their attention on being successful in their own personal lives and their careers. Self-development and personal growth of each person takes on a greater priority. They become more aware of patterns of interaction that don't work and their part in those patterns. They become aware that they can't change their spouse. They learn to accept their spouse for who they are *and* also for who they are not. They must learn to be responsible for what they want, make requests and negotiate with their partner so that they are mutually satisfied. It is incumbent on both partners to learn to communicate well and to bring self-awareness to the task of finding solutions that will work for both of them. Couples who are successful learn to resolve conflict, solve problems and communicate their needs and wants effectively with each other.

When things are not working, they learn to recognize their disempowering points of view or limiting beliefs, to be honest about the cost of those points of view to themselves and their relationship and to be responsible for that impact. They can be counted on to own their responsibility in how problems are solved and how conflicts are resolved so as to avoid hurting their relationship. If they do harm the relationship or hurt their spouse through either words or deeds, they learn how to apologize and to forgive in ways that restore their connection. They allow time for healing and recommit to nurturing their relationship. They learn that taking care of the quality of their marriage *is* the work of marriage. They know that marriage only works in a context of "you, me and us." They ultimately get committed to their commitment to accept each other, grow together and work together to be successful in being partners in their marriage.

Central Conversations in Phase Three

In phase three of a partnership marriage, you and your spouse can have conversations that allow you to be responsible for your contribution to areas of your life that are both working and not working. You can become aware of disempowering patterns of thinking and behaving and see their impact in your interactions with each other. You can design rules for "fair fighting," negotiate agreements to your mutual satisfaction and schedule meetings for effective problem solving. You can also learn to complete hurts in your relationship through the power of apology, forgiveness and recommitment. The conversations in this chapter allow you to expand your awareness of your role in the problems you encounter with each other, solve those difficulties with greater ease and effectiveness and, ultimately, have success in your marriage.

Having all Four Feet in the Ring. In the first years of marriage, you and your spouse may encounter difficulties in communication, misalignment around parenting, conflict about money, inequality in sharing power, problems in intimacy, a lack of trust, etc. When such difficulties remain unresolved for periods of time, it is sometimes easy for you to lose hope or get discouraged and start questioning your commitment to your marriage. You may ask yourselves, "Is this it?" It can be attractive to think that you would not encounter these difficulties in another relationship. It may be easy to think, "I'll step out of this relationship and I'll be happier in another one." The struggle and the courage to create partnership require keeping both feet (in this case, all four feet) in the relationship and staying committed to the vision of a fulfilling and successful life together.

Often when I work with couples at this phase of their marriage, I will ask them to give me a sense of their relationship by simply standing on the large rug in my office and showing me their relationship by positioning themselves on the rug. The rug represents their marriage. More often than not, one or both of them will have one foot on the rug and one foot off the rug. It becomes painfully obvious to the couple that they don't have all four of their feet in their marriage. I suggest to them that having any part of themselves out of their marriage, even if it is only their big toe, will not work in having a happy and successful marriage.

If learning to have a successful marriage is learning to negotiate effectively, communicate directly and handle conflict fairly, etc., doing any of those activities while one or both of you has one foot out of the relationship is very difficult. It is next to impossible for you to create partnership. At best, you will find yourselves sitting on the fence, waiting to choose, "Am I in or am I out?" "Am I committed or not?" Having all four feet in the relationship is a prerequisite for creating partnership. Imagine two boxers in a heavyweight match in which one of the boxers has one foot out of the ring or is straddling the ropes. No matter how good that other fighter might be, he does not know whether to attack, lay back, appeal to the referee or stop all together. The fighter who is straddling the ropes is ambivalent and unsure of himself, ready to leave. Without both of you having all four feet firmly in your marriage, "learning to fight fair" is virtually impossible. Many couples who go into marital therapy do so to resolve the fundamental issue of whether they are "all in" and committed to keeping all four of their feet in their marriage.

When you both have all four feet in your marriage, you are "standing together" for your partnership and for your life together. You can better see what's going on in your relationship and work together to create the life you want. Your marriage is strong and your partnership becomes effective. After powerfully choosing to be fully in your marriage, you both can create whatever future you envision.

Fighting Fairly. When arguments and conflicts occur in your relationship, having ways to "fight fairly" is very important. Fighting fairly means that both of you have a mutual interest in taking care of the relationship as you work out whatever differences you have. The intent of a "fair fight" is to allow you to work out your differences in a context of respect and understanding. The conversation might be difficult, emotions might get heated and feelings get expressed, but nobody gets hurt. You can have an understanding that neither of you ever intend to hurt the other. If one of you does say something that hurts, however, you can quickly see that you crossed the line and then can take the necessary steps to repair the injury to your partner by offering an apology. If you fight fairly, the person who does get their feelings hurt can more quickly see what happened, the intent of their partner and express forgiveness. Examples of fair fighting are:

- Commit to each other that all arguments and conflicts can be resolved through communication and by understanding each other.
- Be committed that the quality of your relationship is always more important than being right.
- Have an agreement that expressing anger by becoming physically violent has no place in your relationship.
- Have an explicit and expressed intent to do no harm and to inflict no emotional hurt.

- When an argument or a conflict gets heated, agree that either of you can call a "time-out," signaling "now is not the time to talk" and that you will talk about the issue at a later time. This agreement allows you both to turn the heat down. When you are both calm, you will pull out your calendars and find a time in the week when you can talk about the issue.
- When you finally do meet to discuss the issue, agree to stay focused on that one issue and not on other issues as well. If other issues arise, agree to put them on a piece of paper and find time to talk about them at a future time.
- Agree to be respectful, kind and understanding.
- Have it be okay to disagree with each other.

Solving Problems by Using "And." Often, couples think that a happy marriage is a problem-free marriage—and a "good" marriage should be free of problems. Let's check this out. Engage in the following little guided tour:

Imagine being together over your entire lifetime. Envision all the things that are going to happen over the next 5, 15, 35 or 50+ years. Imagine all the bills you are going to pay, all the shopping trips, all the vacations, all the activities with your children, all the times you move, all the jobs you will have, all the people you are going to interact with, etc. Now, imagine the entire time being problem-free with your spouse. Envision the perfect life together, problem-free. During your very long life, imagine your marriage having no problems whatsoever. More than fifty years together and no problems in your marriage! You have done it! You have the perfect, problem-free marriage! Now get how absolutely ludicrous that idea is!

You may find the idea of having a problem-free marriage now ridiculous, but it is also worth considering that, when you and your spouse are experiencing a set of circumstance that are problematic for you, you may think that *that* problem should *not* be in *your* marriage. The good news is that you have the power to shift the way in which you speak about those circumstances, thereby, potentially taking a problem and disappearing it *as a problem* for you. First, consider that one way that you can create problems is to use the words "but" and "because" in your conversations about the circumstances in your lives. An example might be, "We want a new car, but we only have $500 dollars saved in the bank." Another way to say it is, "We can't buy a new car because we only have $500 saved in the bank." Using "but" and "because" takes a set of circumstances and makes them appear to be problematic.

Now consider a way you can make a problem disappear or a set of circumstances not problematic: Use "and" instead of "but" and "because" when you talk about your circumstances. For example, "We want a new car and we have only $500 dollars saved in the bank." Or, "We only have $500 saved in the bank and we don't have enough money to buy a new car." Using "and" takes a set of circumstances and makes them seem less problematic. Using "and" allows you to see what is "true" about a situation and what you may be saying about it that is not as true as you first thought. For instance, it may be true that you only have $500 saved in the bank. You might feel as though you can't buy a new car, though in discussing it further, you may see that if buying a car is important enough to you, you may begin to see other possibilities. All kinds of ideas may present themselves. You could take out a loan or borrow the money from a relative. You may consider buying a used car as a short-term solution or you may reconsider whether or not you even need a new car. A set of circumstances that were viewed initially as a problem transforms into a situation that is not a problem to be fixed, but rather an opportunity to explore together. You now have greater freedom to have a conversation around the set of circumstances that initially seemed challenging, difficult and problematic at the start.

Expanding Your Self-awareness. Being aware of your role and responsibility in the quality of your relationships is paramount to being able to have great relationships with people generally and an enduring, loving partnership with your spouse specifically. Self-awareness begins with considering yourself as being at the origin of the quality of your life. If you have many relationships and most of them don't work, you may, at some point, recognize that you are the common denominator in all your relationships. If many areas of your life are not working, you are the common denominator. That realization allows you to begin to observe or examine who you are, what points of view you have and what you are doing that is related to how your life is going. If your relationship with your spouse is not working, ask yourself first what you might have to do with it. The answer starts with self-awareness. Look at yourself before you start looking at your partner. What point of view are you attached to and being right about? How are you being or what are you doing for which you're not being responsible? What impact are you having that you may not be able to see? If your spouse is not happy, what are you committed to?

At this phase in marriage, if you are having difficulty accepting something about your spouse or how your marriage is going, you may start to be aware that there is a way that you are being that is contributing to your unhappiness. Just below the surface of your judgments, attitudes and assessments, there is a framework through which you may be viewing your circumstances. That framework is called "I'm right." Of course your point of view is valid and always has a particular "rightness" to it, given that it is the only point of view you can have at any particular moment in time. The difficulty in your relationship begins when you become attached to your viewpoint as *the* right point of view. "I'm right that I am right." Or "I am right and you are wrong!"

"I'm right, you're wrong" is a perspective that creates problems in your relationship. When one of you makes your partner wrong, the cost to your experience of being in relationship is significant. The costs include a loss of affinity, a breakdown in communication, a closing down of self-expression and a loss of connection. At the moment that "I'm right, you're wrong" occurs, the experience of being related or your sense of "us" disappears. In other words, you can't be right about being right and have an experience of being lovingly related to your spouse at the same time. At that moment, there is no compassion or appreciation for your spouse's point of view. They are just wrong.

The world of "right-wrong" creates a world of "me or you." There is little commitment to understanding each other. There is only interest in being right, being justified or dominating your partner with your point of view. The problem is that to have a happy and healthy relationship *and* marriage, this way of being doesn't work. Having to be right drives a wedge in your relationship and fosters disconnection in your marriage.

When Martha and I quarrel, almost without exception, we are each being right and making the other person wrong. We like to recount the time when Martha came home from the grocery store, having bought hot dogs for a cookout and forgetting to buy hot dog buns. I said, indignantly, "You forgot to buy hot dog buns." She said, "You go shopping next time." She then marched out the door, got into the car, and backed out the driveway. She didn't notice that the backseat door was still open. The door caught the side of the house and, with a loud scraping noise, contorted backwards, twisting off its hinges. I rushed out of the house, Martha got out of the car and we were in a full-blown argument. We were in the world of "right-wrong" and "you or me." I forced the door shut, she stormed off to get hot dog buns, and our nice afternoon cookout was in serious jeopardy. When she returned from the store twenty minutes later, we each recognized quickly that we'd been making each other very wrong. We apologized and forgave each other and went about preparing the food for the grill.

114

So, what do you do when you see yourself being right and the quality of your relationship appears to be suffering (e.g., there's a loss of connection, self-expression and happiness)? What works is to be more committed to understanding each other than being right or justified in your point of view. In other words, you give up being right. You don't have to give up your point of view; you just need to give up being attached to your point of view. You give up *being right* about being right! You may very well have a valid point of view, but holding tightly to it gives you no room to hear or understand your partner's valid point of view. When you give up your attachment to your point of view, you create room for both points of view to be heard and considered. At that moment, being related to each other occurs powerfully because you each see that you are not your point of view, you simply have one.

If you can observe that you simply *have* a point of view rather than being attached to your point of view, you can then examine it, alter it or have a whole new way of seeing something that includes both your points of view. No one has to be wrong. The impact will be understanding, connection and affinity, love and respect and an enhancement of the quality of your relationship with each other.

Another related pattern of thinking that seems to be prevalent in this stage of marriage is the thought that, "If you changed, I'd be happy." "If my wife would only lose more weight, I'd be happy." "If my husband would just do more of the housework, I'd be happy." To say these things, you once again are making your spouse wrong and putting the responsibility for your happiness outside yourself. Wanting your spouse to change sends the signal that your partner is not okay the way they are. The impact of this way of thinking is that your spouse will likely feel hurt, angered and unloved.

When you can accept your partner for who he or she is *and* is not, you send a message that you love and accept your partner unconditionally. In that moment, you both experience love for each other. In fact, nothing needs to change about your partner. What shifts is the perspective that there is anything wrong. When you both are creating that there is nothing wrong with each other and your relationship, you experience being in a state of wholeness. You experience your relationship as working even if you have issues and problem to deal with! You have a joint recognition that you have shared difficulties, not a "problem relationship."

When something is not working as well as you would like in your relationship, another pattern of behavior that you can get into is to start blaming each other. Blame is pointing the finger at your spouse and saying that somehow they are responsible for the problem, difficulty or a set of circumstances that is not working for you. You become unhappy with something that has happened and then find fault in your spouse by blaming them for the situation. Ultimately, there is no responsibility in blaming your spouse. The impact of blame is that it typically creates a defensive stance and a pulling away emotionally on the part of your spouse. Rather than engaging your spouse in getting an issue resolved, the act of blaming often escalates into argument, conflict or withdrawal.

Blaming and defensiveness displaces your responsibility for resolving the issue at hand. When you don't stay with the facts of a situation, share how you feel, state your needs or make requests, you will likely find yourself engaging in mind reading, making faulty judgments or being critical of each other. There are specific patterns of interaction that will stymie any of your attempts at problem solving. Personalization involves attacking your partner rather than the problem by using "you" messages. Rather than separating your partner from the problem, they "become" the problem. The two most common forms of personalization are labeling ("You *are* stupid") or generalization ("You *never* listen to me"). Another obstacle to effective problem solving is leaving the topic of discussion by bringing up other past problems or by bringing up another issue unrelated to the issue at hand. Many times, you might find yourself doing this to defend yourself and to go on the offensive if you are feeling attacked. This strategy could be called "attack and counterattack." Lastly, another way to stymie effective problem resolution with your spouse is to use polarizing language, such as expressing things in language that is "black and white" or "all or nothing." Other examples of polarizing language are "right vs. wrong," "always vs. never" and "truth vs. lie."

Gottman (1994) distinguishes two kinds of unstable marriages where a high degree of hostility is present: The hostile, engaged marriage and the hostile, detached marriage. In both kinds of marriages, there are high degrees of criticism, blame and contempt. The hostile and engaged marriage is characterized by frequent argument, name-calling, putting each other down, being sarcastic and emotional volatility. In contrast, withdrawing from and avoiding each other, not listening to each other, not looking at or even acknowledging each other and detaching emotionally characterizes the hostile and detached marriage. Gottman (1994) refers to criticism, defensiveness, contempt and withdrawal as "the four horsemen of the apocalypse" and are critical warning signs indicating that a marriage has become hostile and is in serious trouble. He has found that such destructive behavior "cascades" in an order of the least to the most dangerous for the well-being of a marriage: Criticism, defensiveness, contempt and withdrawal.

Criticism is a shift from complaining about someone's actions to criticizing the person's personality or character, which is referred to as an "ad homonym attack." Gottman (1994) found that a little criticism is healthy in marriage if it starts an effective conversation for solving an issue to the mutual benefit of both parties. Long-term criticism or continual unresolved complaints, however, can be devastating to the health and well-being of marriage. Criticism that is destructive devolves into bringing up a long list of complaints from the past ("kitchen sinking") and making repeated accusations.

Criticism leads to defensiveness on the part of the other person. Defensiveness is the reflexive, protective reaction to criticism. The problem is that it escalates almost every conflict. Signs of defensiveness are denying any responsibility, making excuses, disagreeing with the other person, withdrawal and counterattack.

Contempt goes a step further than criticism to intentionally insult and to psychologically abuse one's partner. Through contemptuous behavior such as engaging in insults, name-calling, sarcasm and body gestures communicating disgust, a couple experiences a breakdown of trust, love and respect. Finally, withdrawal, like defensiveness, starts with disengaging from meaningful interaction and escalates to terminating any communication at all. Silence prevails. Habitual withdrawal, called stonewalling, can be devastating to the quality of one's marriage.

At the root of such toxic behavior in any marriage, including your marriage, is being right and making your partner wrong, rather than looking at "what is happening" or the facts of the circumstances. If you are engaged in such behavior, you display a fundamental *lack of responsibility* for getting troublesome situations resolved. In fact, you might see that, at the moment of complaining about a situation or blaming your partner for some circumstance in your marriage, you are more interested in being right than in being responsible for resolving your complaint.

If you can learn to give up being right and making your partner wrong and deal with the facts of any situation, you will learn to suspend any tendency to blame or find fault when things aren't working. You will be able to create greater peace and harmony in your lives and deal powerfully with difficulties and problems as they arise. Your orientation will not be who is wrong and who is to blame, but what is not working and how can we address the issue together. You become aware that blame and fault disconnect you, while being responsible for what's not working allows you to connect with each other around what is important to you. As you

118

share with each other what is not working in your marriage, you are able to discern what it is you both need to have the situation be workable. It might be a new perspective, an agreement, a request, a promise or some action that restores wholeness to your relationship. By fostering connection and teamwork and by communicating effectively, you can nurture your relationship.

It will take courage and determination for you to have conversations to create workability in your marriage. As you communicate with each other, effective and powerful actions will reveal themselves. New ways of working together in partnership will be possible. You will find you and your partner on the same playing field of life *in conversation* with each other. You will be responsible and effective in the actions that you take. You will see that to be human is to be ordinary, i.e., to have to be right, to make each other wrong, to withdraw from communication or to let fear stand in the way. By discerning ineffective patterns of thinking and behaving, you can experience being extraordinary together in the way in which you deal with life's challenges!

Scheduling Meetings to Resolve Issues that Arise. Issues and problems are a natural part of life and, in this context, a natural part of marriage. An enduring, fulfilling marriage over a lifetime is not a marriage that is free of conflict, disagreement or argument, but rather one in which both persons in the relationship get their voices heard and their needs met, while at the same time take care of their relationship. When something is not working for you in your marriage, set a time to speak together to get the issue resolved. Remember, the issue might be a concern for only one of you. But if one of you has an issue, there is a problem for the two of you to resolve.

I can remember, learning at this phase in my marriage, that, if Martha had a problem in our marriage or was not happy about something, I needed to listen to her and work with her to resolve the issue for *both* of us. Marriage is a "you and me" phenomenon.

119

With that as our framework, we got in the habit of setting time aside to solve issues or difficulties that arose during the week. Here are some suggestions for allocating time to meet to engage in successful problem resolution:

    a. Create an effective atmosphere to discuss the issue. It is important for you to learn to build the time and the space in your busy lives when you can both sit down to resolve issues. Take the time to have a conversation to discuss what works for you. What time during the week would be long enough and free enough from outside distractions to allow for an effective conversation? What time would work for both of you? It works to have an agreed-upon time in your week that is set aside for such discussions, for instance, on Sunday nights. If an issue is pressing and needs to be discussed sooner rather than later, you can find a time during the week. Each of you can pull out your calendar to find a time when you can discuss the issue and not be interrupted.

    It is also important to find a mutually agreeable location that will support your discussion. Where is there a place in your home which helps you feel empowered to work effectively on the issues? Where is there a place where you can be connected in partnership rather than in a "you vs. me" context? The bedroom will likely not be the best place to talk about difficult issues. The living room, though, where both of you can be relaxed or the kitchen table where you can work together may be better places for you to come together to talk through and resolve problems.

    Having a pad of paper or an easel to write on is crucial. Creating an agenda before you start talking about your issue can help you to focus the discussion and keep you on track. If other issues arise during your discussion, agree to talk about them at another time. What ground rules do you need to put into place to be able to have an effective conversation? You might agree that there is nothing wrong with your relationship, agree to disagree and agree to be respectful of each other's perceptions of the issue and each other's needs. Turn off your cell phones, don't answer your home phone and structure your time in a way that leaves you both free of distractions.

b. Clarify the issue for the two of you. Before you start solving a problem, articulate what the issue is for both of you. This can take the form of: "The issue we are resolving tonight is_____." Being clear about the problem you are discussing can greatly help you to stay focused and be successful.

c. Clarify the intention for meeting together. Before you start solving an issue or resolving a conflict, state your intention for meeting together. This can take the form of: "Our intention today is to_____." By clarifying your intention, you are able to align on what you plan to accomplish by the end of the meeting and/or how you intend to be with one another during your meeting. An example of an intention might be to say: "Our intention is to solve the problem together and to be satisfied with our discussion, clear about where we stand and aligned about what we need to do."

d. Go into your toolbox. Use all the problem-solving tools that are at your disposal.

- Create a context of partnership with each other. For instance, "We are a team" or "We are partners."
- Be committed to listening to and understanding each other.
- Have a conversation about what is important to each of you and your relationship.
- Examine what is not working presently and what would work for both of you with respect to the issue you are discussing.
- Let your partner know how you feel, what you need and what request(s) you may have.
- Be committed to finding a mutually satisfying resolution to the issue you are discussing.

e. Commit to using compassionate communication. Use the four basic components of compassionate communication proposed by Rosenberg (2005):

- Observe what's actually happened in the situation that is affecting your well-being. In other words, observe and acknowledge "what is so" about the situation without making anything wrong.
- State how what happened impacted each of you. Say what you felt in relation to what you observed. Articulate what you are feeling without justification or story.
- State your needs, values or desires that are connected to the feelings that you are having. Tell each other what needs are going unmet, what values you feel are not being honored and what desires are being unfulfilled.
- Make specific requests of each other that address what you each want and desire from your partner.

f. Develop an action plan that is doable and mutually beneficial. Make commitments around what action(s) you each will take and note who is going to do what. Set up a way to be accountable to each other for what you say you are going to do. Schedule a time to reconvene, review what actions have been taken and what actions were not taken and review accomplishments. Also, use this time to clear up any misunderstandings and any promises that have not been kept. Engage in the question: What actions need to be taken, who is going to take those actions and by when?

g. Appreciate each other and what you have accomplished. It is important that you take the time to appreciate and acknowledge what you have accomplished, the ground you have taken and/or the issues that you have resolved. Engage in the question: What have we accomplished and what do we appreciate about each other and our relationship?

Healing Hurts in Your Relationship. There are times in every relationship when couples say (and do) things that are hurtful to each other and trigger feelings of anger, upset, disappointment, frustration, etc. At these times, a couple will often experience a break in connection or in being related. When one person is feeling hurt and angry as a result of what their partner either said or has done, the sense of "us" is disrupted for both of them. If the person who said or did the hurtful thing can recognize that their action had a hurtful impact on their partner, whether they intended that impact or not, it is important that they make an effort to restore their connection by being responsible for the impact their behavior had on their spouse.

Couples who learn to express their feelings in responsible ways, to resolve conflict, to heal hurts and to restore love and wholeness in their relationship have a great advantage in living a life of fulfillment and partnership. Couples who are committed to partnership learn powerful tools that restore their relationship to wholeness when hurtful things are said or done. Those tools are apology, forgiveness and making promises (or recommitting to promises) to engage in behavior that nurtures the relationship.

In the summer of 2008 when Martha and I were vacationing in Amsterdam, we decided to rent a car and drive to the Black Forest in Germany for the weekend. We had always heard that this region of Europe was stunningly beautiful. The morning of our departure, we went into the city to rent a car and then drove it back to our hotel to finish packing and to get ready to leave. As I was packing the car, I said to Martha, "Please check the bathroom. I think I left my antacids on the shelf." For a number of years, I have been taking antacids to relieve the symptoms of heartburn and acid indigestion.

We got on the road late in the morning and drove to Cologne on the western border of Germany where we planned to have dinner and stay in a hotel overnight before traveling on to Freiburg in the Black Forest the next day. It was a beautiful sunny day and we had a wonderful drive across the eastern part of The Netherlands. We couldn't help but think of the Allies during World War II engaging the Nazis in the fields and forests we passed as we drove to Cologne.

We arrived in Cologne late in the afternoon. Although I studied German in college, I couldn't speak the language at all then and I was no better on this trip. That evening, after Martha and I had strolled around Cologne for a bit, we went into a local restaurant where we wanted to order real German food. I opened the menu and ordered the one thing I recognized. "Wiener Schnitzel und bier," I said confidently to the waiter.

As we waited for our dinner to come, I thought I had ordered a German sausage and, of course, it would be coming with sauerkraut. The waiter brought our meals and placed before me a huge piece of fried veal that filled the entire plate. The Wiener Schnitzel was served with a lemon, as is the custom, and with either boiled potatoes or German potato salad. I thought, "Well, this isn't what I thought it was, but it looks good." Martha and I enjoyed our dinner, walked around the city a bit more and then headed back to the hotel around 9:30 PM. We wanted to get off early in the morning.

I awoke in the middle of the night with a sharp stabbing pain in my chest. I first thought, "I must be having a heart attack!" My chest was on fire. I then thought, "Heartburn!" I got up to get my antacid, but I couldn't find it. I was a bit frantic, as I didn't know where Martha had put the medicine the day before. I was experiencing an awful searing pain in the middle of my chest. I knew that I couldn't drink water because water would only make the symptoms of heartburn worse.

My cursing and general state of agitation woke Martha. I was about to wake her anyway. I said, "Where's my antacid? I can't find it." She looked through my belongings and couldn't find it either. I became convinced that she had lost my medication! I then erupted and said something to Martha that was ugly, profane, nasty, accusatory and unforgivable. I can't remember exactly what I said nor do I ever want to. What I said to her, though, was mean, really mean. Martha, hesitated for a moment, put on her robe and left the room without uttering a word.

I lay there in bed thinking that I was going to die, now either from my heartburn or at the hands of my wife. She had every right to walk back into that room and simply announce, "We are done. I want a divorce." I lay there for what seemed like an eternity. I heard the doorknob turn and Martha walked back into the room carrying a large glass of warm milk. It is milk that helps the symptoms of acid indigestion and heartburn subside when nothing else works. As I drank the warm milk, I thought, "I am a real horse's ___." She asked me how I was feeling with genuine kindness, somehow compartmentalizing the impact my words had had just before she'd left the room. I looked her in the eyes and we both knew that tomorrow morning was the time we would need to address the mess I had made of our little weekend jaunt to Germany. As I turned over in my bed, my indigestion and heartburn began to lessen. The dread I felt in anticipation of the morning, however, loomed large.

I awoke in the morning with no physical pain, only with a pain of a very different sort. Martha was already in the bathroom brushing her teeth. She was at the sink in front of a wall-to-wall mirror. As I walked into the bathroom behind her, our eyes met in the mirror. Her stare was cold and icy. Silence hung there in the bathroom as she continued to face the mirror, looking at my reflection as I stood in the doorway.

I walked over to her and said, "Right now, I only have one thing I want to say and I know what I'm going to say will not come close to touching the hurt that what I said caused you. I am very sorry for what I said to you last night." I then walked out of the bathroom. I knew that there was nothing else for me to say at that moment. I also definitely knew that Martha was not interested in talking to me.

I showered and got dressed. Martha showered, got dressed and went back into the bathroom to put on her make-up while I packed up my suitcase. As I packed, I found the antacid exactly where I had put it when Martha had given it to me when we left Amsterdam the day before. When I walked back into the bathroom, I let Martha know I had found the medication. Our eyes met. All there was to say was that I was sorry, again. So, again, I said to Martha, "I am sorry." We gathered our things and headed for the door without saying a word.

As Martha reached for the door handle, I said, "Wait. Martha, I am truly sorry. I know my apologies are not enough. I hurt you deeply with what I said last night. Here is what I want you to do today. At any time during the day today, if you have something you need to say to me, I want you to stop and say what you need say to me. Say it straight. I promise to listen and to get whatever you have to say to me." She said, "Okay" and out the door we went.

We had a lovely drive south to Freiburg for much of the day. We talked some about our plans over the next couple of days, but our conversation was a bit constrained. We arrived in the middle of the afternoon, checked in and went our hotel room. As we unpacked, Martha turned to me, looked me straight in the eyes and said, "Andy, I'm so angry with you! What you said was mean." As Martha spoke to me, I just listened her. I simply said, "I get it." She turned to finish unpacking, as did I, and after a few minutes, she asked me, "What do you want to do?' We talked and decided to walk around the city and find a place to eat.

126

Freiburg is a very welcoming and warm little city. We were happy we were there. The temperature between Martha and me, however, was still pretty cool and we both knew there were still things that needed to be said. Dinner that night did not include Wiener Schnitzel. After dinner, as we strolled around Freiburg, Martha stopped me again. Looking me squarely in the eyes, she said, "Andy, I'm still angry. You are so unbelievably self-centered. What you said really hurt." Holding her gaze, I let her know that I heard her. "I know," I said. I knew that there was nothing for me to say so I kept my mouth shut. I only wanted to make sure that she knew I had heard what she had said to me and was registering just how angry she was.

The next day, we headed toward the Black Forest. For me it was reminiscent of the forests of New Hampshire. The drive was spectacular. We stopped along the way to see vistas that included dark expanses of trees across valleys shrouded in mist and haze. Late in the morning, we stopped for lunch at a park restaurant with an outdoor, grassy patio with tables and chairs overlooking the dense, black forest. We ordered and, as we sat waiting for lunch, Martha leaned over to me as if she was going to tell me a lifelong secret and said, "I'm still pissed at you!" As I listened to Martha, I had a sense that her spirit now was unconstrained. She continued looking me straight in the eyes. I could feel her power. Then she said, "You are a pathetic little dweeb." The image of a dweeb just sat there between us for a very long, pregnant moment. We held that image together for a couple of minutes as we looked into each other's eyes. Martha knew that I understood how angry and hurt she had been. Then, in amazement, we burst into laughter, being cleansed by that healing elixir that once again connected each of us to the whole of us. We laughed and laughed. We then spontaneously hugged each other. Smiling with a twinkle in her eye, Martha said to me, "Pathetic little dweeb. Pretty good, don't you think?"

Tearful and smiling, I looked at Martha and said, "I am sorry. I am deeply sorry for what I said and I will never say anything like that to you again in my life." She smiled back, letting me know that she had accepted my apology, she had forgiven me and she had accepted my promise never to do that again. As the waiter served us our food, I am sure she was wondering what all the smiling and crying was about. The haze and mist lifted, sunlight filled the forest and brilliant colors returned. In that moment, the Black Forest was not as black as it had been when we arrived. In the four years since we were there, Martha and I speak about the Black Forest in Germany as one of the most beautiful regions in the Europe. We hold very fond memories of our weekend visit there.

Being sorry for what you have said or done that has hurt your partner's feelings must come out of your commitment to restore wholeness in your relationship. The expression of being sorry must be in relationship to your understanding of the degree of hurt experienced by your loved one. When you apologize to your partner, you must be able to do so in a way that acknowledges the hurt and pain they're experiencing, acknowledges your responsibility in the matter and expresses your intention to restore the loving connection between you. It is both an expression of responsibility for what happened, whether consciously intended or not ("I know that what I said or did hurt you"), and of a commitment to the restoration of the well-being to your self, your partner and your relationship.

If you have said or done something offensive to your partner, to begin the process of restoring your connection with them, you must be contrite, apologize and say, "I am sorry," with a commitment that your partner understands that you realize the degree of hurt your behavior had on them. If your partner does not get that you have really registered how hurt or upset they are, they are likely not to accept the apology. Saying "I am sorry" is declarative in nature with no expectation for forgiveness. It is an expression of your commitment to the wholeness of your relationship and an implicit request for your spouse to forgive you.

When your apology is offered, however, forgiveness may not be immediately or freely given. Your partner must feel that the apology is heartfelt and may need to say or express their feelings so as to be heard. When your partner is ready to forgive you, *they* are ready to make your relationship whole again. "I forgive you" is a very powerful act. If you are the partner who has been hurt, being able to forgive usually can only occur when you experience that your partner fully understands the impact of their behavior and shows honest and heartfelt contrition. You recognize that your partner has taken responsibility for their behavior, has expressed their commitment to the wholeness of your relationship and has said, "I am sorry" with no expectation of forgiveness from you.

The act of forgiveness creates a new future for your partnership and marriage. When your partner forgives you, they give up the right to be resentful or to harbor feelings of punishing you for what you said or did. Saying "I forgive you" is also a promise that forgiveness will continue to be given freely into the future. Your partner's forgiveness is a powerful request, however, for you to promise to cease the offending behavior. Their forgiveness allows you to make a promise that you will not say or do what was offensive again.

Promising your partner not to say or engage in that hurtful behavior again is the third necessary step in completing hurtful interactions. Your promise is freely given and made from a commitment to the well-being of both of you and to the wholeness of your marriage. Once you have made a commitment not to engage in that hurtful behavior and the promise is accepted, the two of you are able to be whole in your relationship again. In so doing, you both give up a host of feelings and thoughts that may have lingered in the relationship, including thoughts of resentment or regret and feelings of hurt, anger or mistrust. Apology, forgiveness and commitment are powerful tools that you, as a committed couple, can use over and over again in restoring wholeness to your relationship and creating partnership in your marriage.

Conversations for Expanding Self-awareness

Below I have provided you a couple of conversations you can have to enhance your awareness of the impact of disempowering patterns of thinking and behavior in your marriage. Visit www.thepartnershipmarriagebook.com/tools and put in the access code "youandme" (no quotes, all lower case) to download The Partnership Marriage Phase Three Toolkit to your computer.

The following conversations are ones you can have with your spouse to explore the impact of having to be right and making each other wrong, of wanting you partner to change in order to be happy or of blaming each other and being defensive in your marriage. As you have these conversations, consider the impact these ways of being and thinking have on the quality of your marriage.

1. Being Right and Making Each Other Wrong. Have a conversation with each other exploring the impact on yourselves and your relationship when you are being right and making each other wrong. Consider these questions:

- In your relationship presently, what are you being right about, holding on to and making your partner wrong about?
- What are the costs to your relationship when either one of you gets too attached to your point of view and is right about it?
- What happens to the quality of your relationship when you make each other wrong?
- What disappears in your relationship when you are more committed to being right than to the quality of your relationship?

131

- What is possible in your marriage when you are more committed to the quality of your life together than being right about your point of view?
- What is your experience of your relationship when you give up being right?

2. Wanting Your Partner to Change. Have a conversation with each other exploring the impact on yourselves and your relationship when you are thinking that your partner needs to change in order for you to be happy. Consider these questions:

- In your relationship at the present moment, what do you want to change about your partner?
- What are the costs to you and your relationship when you are engaged in this kind of thinking?
- What is possible when you are able to accept each other exactly the way you are and the way you are not?
- In this kind of acceptance and love, what is the quality of your relationship and your life together?

3. Blaming Your Partner. Have a conversation with each other exploring the impact on yourselves and your relationship when you blame each other or get defensive about what is going on in your lives. Consider these questions:

- Presently, what are you blaming your partner for?
- What are the costs to your relationship when you blame or find fault with each other?
- What is the quality of your relationship when you avoid blaming each other and take responsibility for what is going on in your lives?
- When you give up blaming each other, what is the quality of your experience of connection, teamwork or partnership in your marriage?

Chapter

7

YOU, ME AND US

CONVERSATIONS FOR ALIGNMENT, BALANCE AND PARTNERSHIP

"To undertake a project, as the word's derivation indicates, means to cast an idea out ahead of itself so that it gains autonomy and is fulfilled not only by the originator, but, indeed, independently of him as well."

–Czeslow Milosz

Phase Four of a Partnership Marriage

For many couples, life events during the first five to nine years of their marriage can challenge their resolve to support each other's happiness and success and that of their relationship. Whether a couple faces financial difficulties, extra-marital issues or communication breakdowns, each person in the relationship must call on their inner resources to renew their marital commitment. In renewing their commitment to each other, a couple comes to discover that the glue that holds them together is, in fact, their commitment to *each other's* happiness, success and personal development *and* to the growth and success of their marriage. As the couple moves into phase four of a partnership marriage, they no

133

longer question their commitment to their marriage: They *are* their commitment.

During this fourth phase of their marriage, a couple is learning to honor their values, to be true to their vision, to balance their work and family life and to be effective partners in their marriage. *The promise and possibility of this phase is for couples to set the stage for an enduring and fulfilling partnership marriage.* Marriage experts have called this stage of marriage a time of reconciliation, awakening, accommodation, acceptance and collaboration. It is a time when neither individual in the relationship is seriously questioning their commitment to their marriage. They have "all four feet in" and the sentiment in their marriage turns to "I am happy with you and our marriage."

In this fourth phase of marriage, a couple has usually worked out their marital roles and household responsibilities. They are successfully meeting their individual needs and the needs of their relationship. They have gained some mastery at being able to communicate, problem solve and negotiate as they balance the demands of their work, home and community responsibilities. In short, the couple is learning to live in partnership.

Couples at this time in their marriage place a higher priority on both the fulfillment of each person's aspirations and the team-work necessary for mutual empowerment and satisfaction. The couple has an understanding that to have their marriage work, they may periodically re-examine their marital roles, household responsibilities and agreements in their marriage. They are clear that each partner must be 100% committed to the workability, the quality and the well-being of the marriage. In this paradigm, each person is looking from the perspective of being responsible for the whole relationship.

Most importantly, each person fully recognizes that they are wholly responsible for their own happiness, success and personal development. Responsibility in this framework is a declarative act of holding oneself accountable for the quality of one's own life. Each person in the marriage is also committed to the happiness, success and personal development of their partner. Within this framework, partners can take a conscious role in supporting the well-being of their spouse and the health of their relationship. Also, they can consciously avoid doing things or not doing things that they know may upset their partner. While being responsible for the fulfillment of their own lives and committed to the fulfillment of their partner's lives, couples can work in partnership to create the life they want for themselves.

Harrar and DeMaria (2007) call this phase the cooperation stage of marriage. It is a time when couples are clear their marital relationship is a top priority. Couples recognize the importance of continually being in communication and of having conversations that allow them to be in alignment, balance and partnership. A couple's investment of time and energy in the first three stages of their marriage begins to pay great dividends as they move into and through the fourth stage. Having put any doubts and concerns about the success and viability of their marriage behind them, they can fully participate in life, take risks together, and take on bigger commitments. Attention turns to raising their children, creating family life, enhancing their careers, and being involved in volunteer, church or community activities. Emphasis turns to being in alignment around what matters most, what they are committed to and what they wish to build for their future.

The possibility of enduring, fulfilling partnership becomes real when a couple recommits to the quality of their marriage and a long and happy life together. In so doing, they create a shared reality of staying married as true partners. Rather than saying there is no back door or "out" in their marriage, the couple comes to realize that there *is* a back door, there always has been one, and they jointly vow to never to walk through it. The couple commits to openness, honesty, truthfulness, respect and love. They share a commitment to stay "in the ring" with each other over the long term. This commitment ushers in the possibility of being partners in life, of having a successful marriage as well as one that is lifelong. The couple commits themselves daily to the fulfillment of what is possible in their lives together, to the expression of partnership in their marriage and to the vitality of their relationship.

Their recommitment to their marriage opens up a whole new paradigm of partnership for the couple. They recognize that their relationship is a co-created phenomenon. They are no longer attempting to fix each other. Each person sees themselves as the origin or the source of the quality of their lives and relationship. They find themselves being generative and creative, committed to working together to create the life they desire. They hold themselves as whole human beings with nothing missing or needing to be fixed. They become resourceful, imaginative, competent, effective and enterprising in dealing with the circumstances of life. With the building of their careers, establishing their home and raising their children, couples can be in this fourth phase for many years before transitioning to the next phase of a partnership marriage.

Central Conversations of Phase Four

In phase four of a partnership marriage, there are conversations that you and your spouse can have that allow you to explore your expression of partnership. You will be able to assess where partnership is strong and where it is weak in your daily lives. In addition, there are conversations you can have to identify and shift disempowering perspectives in your marriage and restore balance in your busy lives. You will learn to be in alignment around the vision of your partnership, the future you are creating and the life choices you are making together. Lastly, I provide a conversational tool for you to design and fulfill "partnership" projects that require the two of you to work as a team to manifest what you want to accomplish.

Transforming Disempowering Perspectives. Your shared view of your life has great impact on the quality of your marriage. Some couples view their lives through a joint perspective of excitement and adventure. There are couples that view their life as hard work requiring much effort, while other couples see their life as easy and carefree. Still, other couples view their life as full of problems that need to be fixed. These perspectives are not necessarily permanent; you can become aware of disempowering viewpoints in your marriage, see the impact they have on your life together and then shift those viewpoints to ones that give you power, freedom and peace of mind. Whatever perspective(s) you have adopted in your lives will shape the reality you share, impact how effectively you take action and influence how satisfied you are in your marriage

In the course of your life together, you and your spouse may not always be able to change the circumstances you encounter. You can, however, become aware of the ways in which you are both viewing your circumstances. You may share an empowering perspective, such as, "Our relationship is working and we can deal successfully with these circumstances" or you might share a disempowering perspective, such as, "We have no partnership in our life and we are not aligned in solving our difficulties." At times, though, you may be operating inside of a disempowering point of view that you are not cognizant of, but it is having a significant negative impact on the quality of your lives. Such an unwitting perspective frames "the way it is." One couple who participated in my partnership course for couples exemplified this.

Michael and Sarah had been happily married for over 30 years. They worked with me because they specifically wanted to bring a greater sense of partnership to the arena of money. They shared with me the following story.

> In our approach to finances, we have had long-standing, diametrically opposed worldviews. Michael's might be summarized as "We are going to be in the poor house unless we save everything that we can." Sarah's worldview about finances might be portrayed as "Spend it and the money will come."
>
> We had essentially come to grips with these opposing viewpoints early in our relationship and found ways to work around them. Michael would try to hide as much money in a retirement fund as possible and swallowed any residual resentment. Sarah would schedule travel vacations and buy gifts, while hiding her guilt behind a veil of optimism and cheerful-heartedness. This disconnection frequently left Michael feeling like a tyrant and Sarah like a misbehaving child. Over the years this "norm" felt like we were managing the issue, mostly focusing on trying to forgive the other person's misguided beliefs, and basically "blessing their little hearts." In our hearts we knew this was not a place to create passion and partnership for the long term; in fact, the issue was the focal point of most arguments.
>
> In being able to identify our disempowering perspectives and their costs to the quality of our relationship, we broke through to a level of partnership that was previously inconceivable to either of us: A level beyond tolerance, and even beyond cooperation. Initially the challenge was separating each other's perspectives (and our own) from "right" and "wrong." Only then were we

able to create a shared perspective as a couple—a stand for transparency, honesty, mutual respect and shared decision-making.

We named this joint perspective "Partners Without Pants," a tag line that immediately recalls the joy of that discovery and points to a sense of humility and humor in our partnership. Ironically, by joining together in true fiscal partnership, we were also able to see the value in each other's perspective: Michael has secured our future while Sarah has supplied the memories along the way. There is a balance and a union where once there were established battle lines and a lot of point counting.

Together, and in partnership, we have gained power over our finances. We have created room for a supportive relationship with our finances and collaboration on what's important in our lives. We can laugh about money or fight when we disagree—just like real partners do. This is the essence of our partnership now in the realm of our family finances.

How your life and your marriage occur to both of you is a function of how you speak about your relationship. As I have suggested before, what you say about each other, how you talk about your marriage and the kinds of conversations you have with each other make all the difference in how you experience the quality of your marriage. You can become aware of the impact of disempowering perspectives on the quality of your marriage. By being responsible for that impact, you can create empowering perspectives through which to view your lives together, thereby gaining mastery in determining the quality of your relationship.

If you have an area of your life that is not working as well as you both would like, you can engage in a very creative conversation in which you can identify your joint viewpoint of that area, see its impact on the quality of your relationship, take responsibility and then create an empowering perspective that will support you.

First, identify the area of your life that is not working for both of you. Examples of such an area could be your spending habits, your evening routine, the children's homework getting done or visiting your parents-in-law. You want to make sure that you are both willing to invent a new perspective from which you could view this area. You both must be willing to have a shift of perspective that could give you greater freedom and choice. Have a conversation with each other about this area in your life. Share together what it is like for you. What do you experience? What do you feel? How do you view that area? Identify what your current perspective is of this area in your life. "We never agree on anything." "Whatever we do never works." "This area of our lives is hard and complicated." Become aware of the impact your current perspective has on that area of your life. Examples of impact might be a loss of affinity, lack of communication, effort, struggle and unhappiness.

In your conversation with each other, begin to consider other perspectives you could take on to view this area of your lives. Create these new perspectives together. Examples could be looking at that problem area in your life from the perspective of being Olympic champions or Superheroes. You could look at your problem area from the perspective of dance partners, teammates, gangsters or lawyers. Play with this. You could be Clark Kent and Lois Lane or Laurel and Hardy. Any perspective you choose has validity. The point of this is to practice getting out of the point of view you are stuck with and stepping into a new frame of mind that could give you new ways of looking at the area of your marriage that is not working as well as you would like it to. See how that area is for you now through a new lens or viewpoint. Choose a new perspective. What is it like for you? What do you experience? What do you feel? How do you see that area now from this new perspective? Articulate what this new perspective is like and the possible impact on your life.

You can invent a number of different perspectives from which to view that area of your life. Then choose the perspective that empowers you both and one that you are willing to take on in the area of life that has not been working as well as you would like. Stand in your new chosen perspective and look at what that is like for you. Share with each other what you see. "We are adventurers learning together how to master this area of our lives. We can explore this area. We don't have to have all the answers." Take a look at how committed you are to this new perspective in your life. Align with each other in your commitment to taking on this perspective 100% and to creating it in your relationship. Identify what actions you each might take to make your commitment real. Create a plan to support each other in being accountable for what you say you are going to do.

When you are able to have conversations to create new perspectives and effective ways of working, you can transform how you deal with situations where you have been disempowered and experienced ineffectiveness. You can have conversations for the kind of partnership you want. You can talk about you what are committed to and what actions you're going to take to produce what you desire in your marriage. When you can envision a future from an empowering perspective, make big requests and promises and follow through on projects or plans of action, you will have access to a fulfilling and enduring partnership in your marriage. You have the power to create the life of your dreams.

Maintaining Balance. For many couples, life in this phase of marriage can seem out of balance at times. You can easily feel

141

that you have too much on your plate and not enough time in the day to get everything done. Managing all your responsibilities and commitments can begin to crowd out your commitment to the quality of your relationship and the well-being of your marriage.

When you feel that your lives are out of balance, your commitments can begin to occur to you as obligations. You feel that you have little choice. "We've *got* to paint the living room. We *have* to remortgage the house. We *need* to get some exercise. We *should* go to the theater more often." Life can begin to seem like an endless "to do" list where priorities become unclear and activities are not getting done. When having choice is no longer evident, it is easy to be reactive and to take on points of view that don't serve you or your relationship. Viewpoints as to "the way it is" can begin to take root. When choice is absent and disempowering perspectives hold sway, it is easy for you to feel out of balance.

There are several actions you can take when you are feeling out of balance. First, have a conversation to identify what areas in your lives are out of balance and where you feel you have little choice. You can assess the various domains of your life—your home, your health, your children, your recreation, your finances, etc.—and determine how satisfied you are in each area on a scale of 1 to 10 and how much choice you feel you have in the various areas of your life.

As discussed in the previous section, you then can identify any shared disempowering perspectives in those areas of your life where you feel out of balance and have a conversation to examine their impact on your sense of connection with each other. By identifying the impact of a shared disempowering perspective, you have greater choice. You can choose to give up a viewpoint that is not working for you and create a more empowering way to view that area of your life. Such a conversation allows you to return to being "at choice" in how you view your life, resulting in a shared experience of greater freedom, power and satisfaction. While you may not immediately be able to change your circumstances, you do have choice over how you view or hold the circumstances of your life together.

You and your spouse can also support each other in all the commitments you have individually. Do the commitments you've made serve or support your relationship and your family? Have you asked your spouse to support you in extracurricular commitments you've taken on, such as volunteering at church, playing golf every weekend or committing to a major educational endeavor? Gaining your spouse's support can make an enormous difference. It is important to have your partner choose with you. If they do, they will more freely support you in such practical activities as picking up the kids at school, making dinners or cutting the grass on the weekend. When you choose "yes" to a commitment, it is useful to remember that for your lives to work together, your partner also needs to say "yes."

On the flip side, you may be engaged in an activity where it would be appropriate to stop. You may feel that what you are doing is no longer important to you. Or, you may no longer be committed to what you were doing. You can learn to say "no" to those commitments that don't serve you. Being responsible for the choices you make will require you to speak to those people who will feel the impact of your choices. Balance can be restored by identifying where you and your spouse experience having little choice, by shifting disempowering perspectives to empowering ones, and by aligning with your spouse around the commitments you are taking on as well as those you are saying "no" to.

Aligning on the Vision of your Partnership. Alignment in a partnership marriage implies that both people are committed to moving in a direction that not only supports each other but also their relationship. If you see yourselves as partners in life, you will tend to be aligned in what matters to you, in your lifestyle, and in your vision for your partnership. You will align your actions and deeds with your words and promises. When something in your life together is not working or is creating a misalignment, you will work together to resolve the issue and to get back into alignment with each other. Over time, you can learn to have conversations to bring alignment to many aspects of your life. Those areas can include your perspectives on the kind of lifestyle you desire, the values you share, the future you envision, the projects you create and committed action you take realize your dreams. Working in alignment engenders trust. Being in alignment, like being in balance, is a mechanism for a couple to be true to their experience of partnership.

An important area where you and your partner can be in alignment is in articulating a vision for your lives and your relationship. A vision for your partnership conveys what you want to express in the world. It is not just the achievement of life goals or objectives. A vision for your partnership could be thought of as the way you envision the quality of your marriage. To envision is "to picture in the mind or to imagine something not yet in existence." It is well recognized that a powerful vision is crucial to inspiring people and providing a direction and a mindset for success (Miser, 2006). Similarly, couples committed to partnership can co-envision the desired quality of their life together and, standing in that vision, take action to bring that vision into reality. Co-creating and being aligned on a vision for your partnership are powerful ways to express your marriage in the world.

Aligning on a Vision of Your Future. Another way you and your partner co-create your lives is through inventing a specific future for your lives. To create the future, you first anchor yourselves in what you value and in the vision your partnership. Then, visualize and share with each other your dreams for the future, irrespective of time. Bring your whole life to the process, looking at the all areas of your life, such as your home, family, friends, community, work, career, retirement, play, recreation and health. As you share your vision of the future, step into those future images and experience what it is like having that future be real for you. Where are you living? How does it feel for you both? What do you experience? What does it look like? What is it that lights you up about what you see?

As you stand in the future you are creating together, you are using the same abilities that Merlin the Magician used as mentor to the great King Arthur of the Round Table. Merlin had a special ability to see the future before it occurred. The process of standing together and visualizing images of the future gives you, as a couple, a magic wand like that of Merlin the Magician. Such a view from the future gave Merlin extraordinary insights into what would happen in the present and what actions he would advise King Arthur to take. Smith (1994) called this "The Merlin Principle." When you use The Merlin Principle, you look *from* the future *to* the present time, which allows you to see, feel and sense your future in a clear and tangible way. Smith (1994) introduced The Merlin Principle in this way: "What you choose for your future is more important than what you know about your past or present capabilities."

Once you share and experience your desired future together, you can choose and align on a timeframe for the manifestation of the future you both have. You can choose a timeframe of 25, 15, 10, 5, or 2 years. Standing together in your co-invented future years from now, you can view the path from that future to the present moment and clearly see what actions you took and what you accomplished along the way. Working from the future (say, 2 to 5 years out) to the present time, you can articulate, in a timeline, the milestones, accomplishments and the actions that naturally occurred on the path to your future. Committing together to the future you have created is an expression of your partnership in action. Almost immediately after making this commitment to your future, you will see a host of "partnership projects" required to fulfill the future you have envisioned.

Sometime after our third child was born in 1991, Martha and I sat down and created fifty-year vision of our future. We imagined our three children going to college and each of them pursing interests and work they love. We envisioned traveling overseas and even talked about living in a foreign country at some point. We thought about what it would be like for our children to get married and for us to be grandparents one day. We discussed having our own businesses and even doing work together. We even imagined being at each other's ninetieth birthday parties! We called that vision "Metamorphosis," because we both knew that to fulfill the future we had designed together would require both of us to change over the years.

Almost twenty-five years later, much of what we saw for our lives that day has come to fruition. And much has yet to happen. Scott M. Stanley (2005), who has studied the power of commitment in marriage, says that a couple who shares and nurtures a vision for their life together lives with a greater sense of fulfillment and prosperity. He wrote that a vision is very important for a strong and healthy marriage. He cites research evidence that suggests that, over the course of their marriage, happier couples talk regularly about their future, whereas unhappy couples do not.

It begs the question, why is vision so important for a healthy and vibrant marriage? A vision helps a couple to view their lives together in the long arc of time. Over their life's journey together, they will share many meaningful experiences, go through necessary life transitions and accomplish many individual and joint life goals. Stanley (2005) suggests that a vision provides a couple with a "long view." The vision that Martha and I created years ago has helped us to shape the life that we have shared to date and will continue to give meaning to our marriage for years to come.

The benefits of taking the long view in your marriage are many (Stanley, 2005). You and your spouse will be better able to nurture a healthy perspective in facing problems together, feel secure in taking risks that will challenge your relationship, have faith that things will work out for the best, invest time and energy in the growth of your relationship and participate in important family traditions that bring continuity to your lives over the years.

Making Powerful Choices. The ability to work together in making important life choices makes a world of difference in how satisfied and how fulfilled you are in your marriage. One powerful way you can participate together in making important life choices is to "Create a Banana List."

My mother-in-law, Ruth, tells a story about her eldest daughter, Amanda, who at a young age would become upset, at times, about having her younger baby sister, Sarah, in the house. Ruth was making breakfast one morning, having put out cereal, milk and a banana for Amanda to eat. Ruth had placed the banana down next to a cereal bowl on the breakfast table. As she attended to Sarah, Ruth looked up and discovered Amanda mashing up the banana with her hands. Amanda was upset that her younger sister was commanding her mother's attention.

Ruth, who in that moment had reached her limit, sent Amanda to her room with a piece of paper, a pencil and explicit instructions. Ruth made two columns with the headings at the top of the paper, "What I like about my life" and "What I don't like about my life." Ruth told Amanda that she was to stay in her room until she had completed both lists.

After a period of time, Amanda reappeared, with her lists. Ruth asked her what she had on her lists. On the "What I like about my life" list, Amanda had written, "my dolls," "Christmas presents," "playing outside," "ice cream," "birthday parties," "my friends," "reading stories" and "the Easter bunny." On the "What I don't like about my life" list, Amanda had written only one item, "mashed bananas." By that time, Amanda had pulled herself together and went off playing happily outside.

In sending Amanda to her room, Ruth had implicitly presented Amanda the choice of being happy or not. In the exercise of creating a list, Ruth had asked Amanda to make that choice by considering all the "pros" (the things she liked) and the "cons" (the things she didn't like) about her life. By the end of her deliberation, Amanda quite naturally had made the choice to be happy. The activity that Ruth had spontaneously presented to Amanda that morning became known in the family as "Creating a Banana List."

"Creating a Banana List" is a powerful tool that you can use to make important choices. By engaging in this activity together, you are able to align powerfully on an important choice confronting you and make a commitment together. Important choices include having children, buying a home, moving, changing careers, creating a business, negotiating family roles, buying or leasing a car, enrolling a child in day care, investing money, choosing a place to worship and planning for retirement. If you have a powerful and effective way to make important life choices, you will find yourselves experiencing peace of mind and trust in your ability to work together in creating the life you envision.

a. Clarifying the choices under consideration. When you and your partner have an important choice to make that will have major ramifications in your lives, give yourselves ample time to consider the specific choice under consideration. Take time to clarify and align on each specific, possible scenario that you might be considering, for instance, "buying the colonial home in Brookline" or "buying the Victorian home in Boston." When making an important choice, such as buying a house, it works to be as specific as you can and clarify each possible scenario you are considering.

b. Discussing all the "pros" and all the "cons" of each scenario. Once you have identified each of the discrete possibilities you are considering, discuss all the "pros" and the "cons" for each scenario. It is important that you allow yourselves to say anything and everything you need to say in this process. Under each scenario, list all the positive aspects (pros) and all the negative aspects (cons) of making that choice. Giving yourselves permission to express your deepest fears, persistent worries and greatest hopes allows you to be honest, truthful and fully self-expressed. As each of you expresses a concern about any of the scenarios, write down those concerns. If either one of you expresses a positive point about any of the scenarios, write down those as well. When all the pros and cons have been communicated for each scenario, sit back and consider your choice together. "Which possible future are we each going to choose?" Discuss the list of pros and cons for each scenario.

c. Making your choice. Making a choice after complete consideration of all the pros and cons of each future scenario is a very powerful act. Many times couples make an important life choice by "deciding" on the basis of a consideration ("because it will be fun") before they have considered <u>all</u> the aspects involved in making that particular choice (e.g., "it is very expensive," "the weather will be overcast most of the time," and "it will be lots of fun"). When every-thing (i.e., all the pros and the cons) has been expressed, each of you can make your own choice, choosing freely and independently of your partner. In this way, each of you can be responsible for what you choose. Given that each of you will have taken the time to com-plete the Banana List deliberately and consciously, it will be easier for you both to accept and deal with any difficulties that arise after you have aligned and committed to a particular path.

d. Aligning on your choice. If you each make the same choice, you are aligned in your commitment. It can be a very powerful, exciting and intimate experience for you both when you have made a spe-cific commitment for your future. Once you are aligned, take some time and share with each other your enthusiasm and even your fears about the new path you have chosen for your lives together.

If you haven't made the same choice, then you are *not* aligned and it is advisable that you continue to discuss your hopes, desires and concerns for the various scenarios you are consid-ering. You can put off making any commitment until some later time after additional thought, consideration and discussion. By giving yourselves more time and by not forcing the choice when you find yourselves not aligned, you might discover other possi-ble scenarios you can consider in another Banana List! At some later date, you can create a new Banana List based on your most current perspectives and possibilities.

Important choices and commitments require your time, energy and a dedication to a process in order to arrive at a choice you can both be responsible for and be happy about. Neither of you want to feel dominated, be unheard or feel as though you have no choice in such important matters. The "Creating a Banana List" conversation gives you a creative process by which you can articu-late the various possibilities under consideration, share all of your concerns, hopes, desires and fears, and make a joint commitment.

Martha and I used the Creating a Banana List exercise to assist us in making one of the most difficult choices we have made in our marriage. In the late winter of 2002, Martha was given the opportunity to consider a new job in Amsterdam, The Netherlands. We were living in Hartford at the time in a beautiful colonial home in the west end of the city where we had raised our three children, had cultivated many friendships and built our professional lives. I was a psychologist and marriage and family therapist in independent practice and Martha was a professional trainer and educator with a financial services corporation. We were well ensconced in the community and I could not for a moment imagine making any significant change until Martha was offered this exciting job opportunity in Amsterdam. To assist us, we created a Banana List.

We generated the Banana List by looking at the pros and cons of the scenarios we had before us. We first wrote down the different possible futures we were considering. For us, it was easy: Make a whole-scale change and move to Amsterdam or stay in Hartford with the life we knew. Martha and I made a rule that we would communicate everything we needed to say about either of these possibilities while we discussed each scenario. We granted ourselves the freedom and the permission to express our deepest fears and worries as well as our hopes and desires. When I expressed the concern that our children might be upset with us in moving to Amsterdam, we wrote that on "Move to Amsterdam" list under "cons." When Martha expressed excitement about traveling in Europe, we wrote that on the same list, but under "pros." After a fairly lengthy discussion, we had all of our concerns and hopes registered for each of the two possible scenarios. Although our lists were much longer and more detailed, they looked something like the table below.

Move to Amsterdam		Stay in Hartford	
Pros	**Cons**	**Pros**	**Cons**
We can travel in Europe	Our children may be upset	We won't have to deal with all the changes	We will still be in Hartford
Living in Europe will be an adventure	We will miss our friends and family	We will be near our friends and family	Life will be predictable
We can ski in the Alps	We will have to deal with all the uncertainty		Martha will give up a once-in-a-lifetime career opportunity
We can learn to speak Dutch	We will miss our beautiful home	We can get to Red Sox games (or see them on TV)	

After considering all the pros and cons, we sat back and asked ourselves the question, "Which path am I (we) going to choose?" We found this to be a very powerful process. We made the choice individually and, fortunately for us, each of us chose to move to Amsterdam. We were aligned and excited about our future. If we hadn't been aligned, we would have gone back to the drawing board.

Making the choice together to uproot our family and to go to Europe was a major, positive step in our expatriate experience. After our family arrived in Amsterdam, Martha and I were better able to be responsible for and to deal effectively with all the adjustment issues our family encountered. As problems arose, Martha and I couldn't blame each other for any of the challenging circumstances in our lives. We had both chosen, in partnership, to move to The Netherlands.

Choosing to move to Amsterdam by using the Creating a Banana List exercise paid off for us over the next four years. Instead of feeling victimized or resentful when things were difficult, we felt we could deal with all the challenges that were facing us without sacrificing our happiness. We were able to be effective in coping with many of the common dilemmas that confront expatriate couples and families: Feeling like you don't belong, dealing with cultural differences, restoring family stability and creating a home in a new country.

Being aligned and responsible for the choice we had made gave us the freedom to fully immerse ourselves in our new lives. I began taking over the household tasks at home, learning to cook, learning to speak Dutch, reading and writing routinely, and designing a whole new career as a professional coach. I also started my own international coaching business. Martha was able to advance her career by working in an international corporation in Amsterdam and we were able to travel with our family to many different countries throughout Europe. Having simply engaged together using the Creating a Banana List exercise and making our choice after careful consideration of all the pros and cons, Martha and I were able to invent a whole new future for ourselves and for our family.

Designing and Fulfilling Partnership Projects. To fulfill a project, by its very nature, requires the partnership of those involved. Partnership projects are distinct from the normal routine of life. In conversation, you and your spouse can "co-create" a project to bring the future you have designed into existence, "co-operate" in fulfilling the project and "co-own" the results of your work together. Partnership projects can be created in any area of life, such as home improvement, financial well-being, children/family, career, education, community or vacation and travel. Projects are designed to be time-limited and have a specific measurable result.

After creating your future using the Merlin Principle, you will find that many projects will start to appear on your joint "radar screen." By designing projects together, you and your partner can cooperate in planned action and in being responsible for your accomplishments; both intended and unintended outcomes. You can examine and acknowledge any disempowering perspectives you may have unwittingly adopted along the way as well as identify actions that you still need to take. Over time, by being responsible for what you are accomplishing, you can continually re-create your partnership and stay in action.

When creating projects and bringing them to fruition, you will find that there are several necessary steps to designing a successful partnership project. These include creating the future accomplishment of the partnership project, sharing any current perspectives and concerns that may be limiting the project outcomes, creating and choosing an empowering way of being for the project, defining the actions necessary to fulfill the partnership project and putting those actions into a project timeline. It also works and is fun to name the project. You will also discover that, throughout the life of your project(s), it is important that you meet periodically so you can evaluate the results of your actions, plan the next steps of your project and be in alignment on a regular basis. Here are the recommended steps to co-create a partnership project:

Step 1. Create what you intend to accomplish in the partnership project. To create a project, you and your partner say what you want to accomplish by writing it down in the following way "Our project is to have (an accomplishment) by (specific time). It is important that the statement is as specific as possible. For example, "Our project is to have our daughter and her fiancé married in a beautiful, loving ceremony in July, 2015, with 180 people in attendance." Or, "Our project is to have traveled to ten major cities in Europe in the next four years." Each project is stated as an expression of the future that you are creating. By stating the project in this way, you can be aligned in what you are building for the future. As described briefly earlier in this chapter, steps two and three outline a conversation you can use to identify disempowering perspectives you may have that are unwittingly framing your project and then to create new perspective that can empower you in your project (Whitworth, Kimsey-House & Sandahl, 1998).

Step 2. Identify the shared current perspectives and concerns that frame the project. The next step in designing a project is to identify any disempowering shared or individual perspectives or concerns that might unwittingly shape your relationship to the project. Such unwitting perspectives might be, "This project is going to be a lot of work and hard to accomplish." Or, "This project is going to put a lot of stress on our family." Or, "The costs of the project will get out of control." By identifying such current perspectives, concerns, worries, perceived barriers or anticipated obstacles, you are able to deal powerfully with them. You can see your initial perspectives about the project and be responsible for your current viewpoint. Write your initial perspectives and concerns in one of the wedges of the Partnership Umbrella Sheet in Appendix 1

Step 3. Brainstorm other perspectives and choose an empowering perspective for your partnership project. The next step of designing a partnership project is to brainstorm a number of different perspectives that could frame the project.

   a. Invent another possible perspective from which to view your partnership project. An example might be, "Our project is an opportunity for collaboration," or "Our project is fun and exciting" or "Our project is inspiring and fulfilling." Look at your partnership project from another shared perspective. How does your project look to you both from this new perspective? What do you feel? What do you experience? Become aware of the impact this perspective might have your project. Write this new perspective in another wedge of the Partnership Umbrella.

b. Invent and examine a number of different perspectives from which to view your partnership project. As you engage in this exercise, write the various perspectives in the different wedges of Partnership Umbrella sheet.

c. When you are ready, each of you choose one of the perspectives in the Partnership Umbrella that empowers you and that you'd be willing to take on in your project. Adopt that new perspective and look at how that perspective shifts your view of your project. Experience what it is like for you looking at your project from this new perspective. Note: If you each have chosen a different perspective, have that be okay. Simply put the two perspectives together and imagine marrying them into one joint perspective.

d. Adopt this new and empowering perspective together as you design the actions and the accomplishment for your partnership project.

e. Design all the aspects of your partnership project (outlined in the next sections) inside of this co-created and empowering perspective.

Step 4. Create the actions and the interim accomplishments necessary to fulfill the partnership project and put them into time. At this point in the project design, you are standing together in your empowering perspective of the project, knowing what you are committed to and imagining yourselves having accomplished your project. Now look from the accomplishment of the project to the present time. Starting from that future accomplishment working toward the present time, brainstorm all the interim accomplishments that will occur during the project and all the actions that will be taken inside the project. As you do this, put the actions and accomplishments in a timeline from the fulfillment of the project to the present time.

One project timeline format that is useful is to write two columns on a piece of paper: Date and Actions/Accomplishments. In the timeline, now working from the present to the future accomplishment of the project, list, in sequence, the specific dates of the actions and accomplishments of your project. You can invent and can use whatever project format works for you.

Step 5. Name the project. Next, give your project a fun name. The name can call forth the perspective of your project, the values you share or the future accomplishment you desire. When Martha and I were moving our family to Boston after our time in Amsterdam, we named our project to find a new home there, "Make Way for the Misers," borrowing from the famous children's book by Robert McCloskey, called *Make Way for Ducklings.*

Step 6. Schedule the project meetings. Once you have designed your partnership project, make a plan to meet on a regular basis and determine the length of your project meetings. In the beginning, it is often wise for you to meet frequently, say once per week for an hour or so, and then meet less frequently or as needed as the project progresses. You will find what works for you both as you engage in fulfilling partnership projects.

In every project meeting, start with creating an agenda. In these project meetings, you can evaluate what you are accomplishing, recommit to your commitment and get into action to fulfill your future. Here is a recommended agenda for project meetings:

a. What is our agenda? Together, create the agenda for the project meeting before getting involved in the meeting content itself.

b. What do we need to let go of to be fully present in this project meeting? Here simply communicate anything you need to so you can fully engage with each other.

c. Who are we as a partnership? Share your core values or express the vision of your partnership. This conversation allows you to get powerfully related as partners as you review the status of your project.

d. What are we creating in this partnership project? Briefly review what you intend to accomplish in the project.

e. What have we accomplished? Share what each of you has accomplished since the last project meeting.

f. What is the current perspective we have for this project? Share anything you see that is a disempowering perspective, concern or obstacle to fulfilling your project.

g. What is the empowering perspective that we created for this project? You can also ask yourselves: What new empowering perspectives do we want to take on in this project?"

h. What are the short-term actions that need to be taken? At this point, work with the project timeline, revising the timeframe, editing the actions and accomplishments and re-aligning aspects of the plan. (If you have the project timeline in a document on your computer, it can be easily and repeatedly updated.) Discuss who will do what and by when. Also, discuss how you want to be in communication with each other along the way. Some aspects of the project can be discussed at the next project meeting while others need to be discussed on an ongoing basis.

i. What do we acknowledge ourselves for? What do I (we) appreciate? Take a few minutes to say anything to acknowledge your partnership or to appreciate each other's commitment, effort and/or actions related to fulfilling the project.

j. When will we meet again? Schedule another project meeting in your calendars.

Conversations for Supporting Your Alignment and Partnership

Below, I have given you a couple of conversations you and your spouse can have to help you be in greater alignment and partnership in your marriage. You can explore what is like when you are in partnership with each other and when you are not. In this conversation you will reveal to yourselves the quality of your shared experience when you are in partnership and when you are not. In addition, I have given you a conversation in which you can share your dreams for the future and share what it provides you in your marriage when you take the long view. You can find additional tools and exercises by visiting the website www.thepartnershipmarriagebook.com/tools and putting in the access code "youandme" (no quotes, all lower case) to download The Partnership Marriage Phase Four Toolkit to your computer.

1. Exploring Partnership. In this exercise, you will explore the "world of partnership" and the "world of no partnership."

    a. Exploring the world of no partnership. First, you will explore what it is like for the two of you when partnership is absent in your relationship. Together think of a time when you were engaged in some activity, such as painting a room or having a dinner party and you both experienced an absence of partnership in your relationship. You want to find a time when you were planning to get something done where partnership was needed, expected or clearly being wanted or called for, but, unfortunately, it was absent. Become aware of that experience. What is the quality of life together when partnership is absent?

Individually, on a piece of paper, jot down what you experienced at that time. If you want, you can close your eyes and imagine you are there in that moment experiencing no partnership. What are you experiencing in your body? What are you feeling?

What reactions are you having? What are you saying to yourself? What assumptions and beliefs do you have? Now share with each other what you each experienced when partnership wasn't present. Other ways that you can do this are to draw a picture of what it is like to experience a loss of partnership with your spouse or to pull out magazines and find pictures that depict what it looks like to have an absence of partnership.

Once you have shared your experience of no partnership through your words, drawings or pictures, each of you name the experience of no partnership. Examples might be "loneliness," "confusion," or "solitary confinement." The names you choose will likely embody the experience you have when partnership is absent in your relationship.

b. Exploring the world of partnership. Next, explore what it is like for the two of you when partnership is present in your relationship. Together think of a time when you were engaged in some activity, such as cleaning up the lawn outdoors or planning a trip together, and you both experienced the presence of partnership in your relationship. You want to find a time when you were planning to get something done where partnership was needed, expected or clearly being wanted or called for, and you experienced being in partnership. Become aware of that experience. What is the quality of life together when partnership is present?

As you each did before, individually, on a piece of paper, jot down what you experienced at that time. If you want, you can close your eyes and imagine you are there in that moment experiencing partnership. What are you experiencing in your body? What are you feeling? What reactions are you having? What are you saying to yourself? What assumptions and beliefs do you have? Now share with each other what you each experienced when partnership was present. Remember, additional ways that you can do this are to draw a picture of your experience of partnership or cut pictures out of magazines that represent the experience of partnership.

Once you have shared your experience of partnership through your words, drawings or pictures, each of you name the experience of partnership. Examples might be "accomplishment," "teamwork" or "fun together." The names you choose will likely embody the experience you have when partnership is present in your relationship.

2. Dreaming Together. Together with your spouse, here are great questions to ask yourselves:

- What future are you building together?
- What are your dreams? (Examples are traveling, playing with grandchildren, writing a book, learning a musical instrument, getting involved in politics, creating a business, etc.)
- What are your goals (financial, marital, family, recreational, educational, career, etc.) individually and together?
- What support do you each request from your partner and need from others?

It is an important investment of time and energy to set aside time to talk about the future you are building together, to share your dreams and your goals and to create plans of action to make your dreams come true. Get out your calendars and schedule time to build your future!

3. Taking the Long View. Imagine your life together forty or fifty years from now. Imagine you are a couple who has been able to manifest an enduring, fulfilling marriage over their lifetime. You have achieved the benefits of a partnership marriage. Look at the quality of your marriage and of your lives together. Standing in the future,

- What is like to have an enduring, fulfilling partnership marriage?
- What did taking the long view in your marriage make possible in your life together?
- What is present is your relationship?
- What is the quality of your lives?
- What are you contributing to other people around you?
- Who have you been for your family and friends?
- What made the difference in your marriage over these past forty to fifty years?

Chapter

8

REINVESTING IN US

CONVERSATIONS FOR PASSION, FULFILLMENT AND CONTRIBUTION

"Only those who have learned the power of sincere and selfless contribution experience life's deepest joy: true fulfillment."
–Tony Robbins

Phase Five of a Partnership Marriage

The fifth phase of a partnership marriage is a time of much transition in life. If a couple has had a family, their grown children are going off to college, entering the work force or, maybe, joining the military. The couple may be completing their career, transitioning to retirement, downsizing their home and wondering a lot about what's next in their lives. Many couples at this stage have been on a long marital journey together. This phase is a time for renewed focus on their marital relationship and has been called the stage of real love and reunion (Harrar and DeMaria, 2007).

In this fifth phase of a partnership marriage couples are looking forward to enjoying each other's company, their adult-to-adult friendships and potentially the prospect of having grandchildren. They begin to orient themselves around what they are passionate about, what fulfills them and what contribution they wish to make in their community. They know it is a time when taking care of their health is vital to being able to fulfill new dreams and those they have been putting off for years. At this stage, couples fall in love with each other all over again and the sentiment in the marriage turns to "I am fulfilled in our life together."

As this phase begins, married couples may feel as though they are living parallel lives and have a yearning to reconnect with each other and rediscover a new purpose for their lives and their marriage. Couples at this time also find themselves in the midst of many life changes. In addition to completion of careers and children leaving home, couples may anticipate the marriage of their grown children, the birth of grandchildren and the death of their parents. Husbands and wives may make major shifts in the roles at home. One partner may be slowing down in their professional life while the other may be interested in pursuing new life paths, such as going back to school and getting a Ph.D. Couples are searching for renewed meaning and purpose in their lives not wanting to settle for work or activities that are not fulfilling. Couples realize that the time is *now* to explore what they really care about. Couples rediscover simple pleasures like working in the garden, traveling and getting together with friends. They also take on projects that require their joint attention, team effort and coordinated activity.

In this fifth phase of partnership marriage, a couple stands together for creating a fulfilling way of living in their marriage. Their marriage is a resource for each partner to reassess their lives, to find their passion and to re-examine their unique contribution. Being partners has become a way a life for the couple. They also have become a beacon for others who want to embark on the journey of having a passionate and loving partnership marriage over a lifetime. Their relationship is a powerful reminder that a long and fulfilling marriage is possible for everyone who chooses that path.

Couples are aware of what it has taken for them to create and share an enduring and fulfilling life together. The focus and the care they have been putting into their marital relationship over the years have given them a platform to make a real difference in their families and in their communities *on their terms*. Their partnership gives them a strong foundation for each of them to step out and contribute in the world. It is not uncommon for couples to seek support groups and/or professional coaches to help them stay true to their renewed purpose. Living lives that are creative, self-expressed and purposeful is important to both partners.

Many people at this stage in life are willing to take big risks, to be vulnerable, to innovate and contribute to their family, community and wider society (Lawrence-Lightfoot, 2009). Older couples want to support each other in continuing to grow and develop in new and exciting ways. For them, being creative and self-expressed is vital to this stage of their lives. Today, baby boomers have entered this developmental stage of life and are re-establishing the rules for living into what used to be called the "retirement years." Retirement today is a euphemism for "what are you up to now?"

One late summer afternoon in 2005 when Martha and I were still in Amsterdam, we sat down to have a conversation about our future. Martha said, "Let's create a collage." My first thought was, "No, let's just talk." After a short time of recalcitrance on my part, I succumbed to her obvious enthusiasm. We pulled out magazines, paste, scissors and a piece of poster board we had in the closet. We tore pictures out of magazines that depicted images of the kind of life we enjoy and what was important to us. After we cut out the pictures and pasted them on the poster board, we put the collage up on the mantelpiece.

With the collage as a framework for our planning, we started talking about, "What's next in our lives?" "What are we now up to?" We chose the year 2017, a twelve-year period, in which we could envision what we wanted to accomplish in our lives. Twelve years was a long time; long enough so our future wasn't necessarily predictable and long enough for us to take a big view of our relationship. As we created our vision of the future, we said what we each wanted to accomplish as well as what we wanted to have together. Our vision also included what we hoped for our three adult children, knowing full well that their lives were theirs to determine. We talked for an hour, typed what we had envisioned and saved it in a Word document on the computer. I had also written and saved some of the words that we had used to describe the quality of life that the images had called forth for us in our collage: Playfulness, being together, beauty, adventure, mystery, inspiration and wisdom. These words still capture the life we are living today!

In phase five of a partnership marriage you have all the conversational tools available to you to support you in living passionately, being fulfilled and making a contribution. You are able to have conversations for intimate connection, for clarifying what you are committed to, for being a team, for solving problems, for being self-aware, for being aligned, for having balance and for being partners. You have a solid commitment to the quality of your marriage and are interested in pursuing your passions and what fulfills you. You and your spouse want to make a difference. You want to contribute. You are partners in living. You know the power and value of being in conversation for creating the life of your dreams...together!

Central Conversations in Phase Five

At this phase of your marriage, there are additional conversations that you and your spouse can master that will allow you to nurture your partnership, redesign family roles with your adult children and aging parents, assess at what crossroads you find yourselves, dream big together, invent a new purpose for your marriage and commit to contributing boldly.

Nurturing Your Partnership. In this fifth phase, couples reinvest in their marriage and put their focus on their partnership (Arp, et. al., 2001). You want to reclaim time for yourselves to nurture your deep friendship, renew your passion, and create romance. It is a time to plan special dates, weekend getaways and fun vacations. It is a time to travel and see the world! It can be particularly fun to go on vacation to exotic lands with other couples you enjoy.

You recognize that life is short, time is now and you give yourself no permission to stay upset or angry toward each other for any length of time. When problems arise, you get into conversation and resolve them. When you need something, you say so. When something is not working for you, you speak up. You don't take yourselves for granted. You are committed to being in conversation regularly.

Jeanne and Richard have been committed to honesty, communication and flexibility in their relationship. They had a special restaurant in their town where they loved to dine and spend the evening in conversation. They shared with me this wonderful anecdote.

> Whenever difficulties arise in our relationship, we sit down and talk and work things out before a crisis occurs (or sometimes, after!). We named our place for honest communication, Bar Louis, after a favorite restaurant where we used to go to eat, relax and talk. It is this place where we can communicate most openly and iron out our issues. We have moved from the town where Bar Louis was located, but that's not a problem. Bar Louis is now a state of mind and we can recreate Bar Louis anywhere and anytime we need it.

Phase five of a partnership marriage is a time to resolve issues quickly and with intention. If you find yourself making each other wrong, you stop because you know the lunacy of such behavior. Martha and I learned this for good one evening in Amsterdam. We celebrated our thirtieth wedding anniversary while we were living there. It was August 10, 2004. For weeks we looked forward to this special day as we were planning to go out to eat at one of our favorite restaurants. That evening, we got all gussied up and, as we were putting on our coats to go out the door, one of us said something (I don't remember what) that sparked bickering back and forth. It could have been an issue with one of our children, a concern about money, or who was going to go shopping for food in the morning.

We bickered down the stairs, out the door, across the street, all the way to the tram stop where we were catching the city tram to go to the restaurant. We were lost in squabbling. I was quite certain that I was right about whatever I was saying and Martha was quite certain she was right about what she was saying. We were so occupied in our verbal sword fight that we had lost track of the whole purpose of what we were doing. We stood there at the tram stop arguing about that very insignificant and ridiculous issue as the tram pulled up and opened its doors.

At that moment, we were both jettisoned back to the present moment. We stood there, looking at each other, as the tram doors beckoned. We simultaneously saw the folly of our situation. We were headed out to dinner to celebrate our anniversary and we were knee-deep in a pile of verbal do-do. There was a long pause. Then, as if by magical combustion, we conjured up a very radical and completely silly idea in our momentary madness. We called, "Do over!"

We turned away as the doors closed and the tram pulled away from the stop and we walked in silence in the direction of our apartment. We crossed the street, climbed the stairs to our second floor apartment, unlocked the door and went upstairs into the living room to the very spot where we had started bickering.

We briefly stood with each other in silence, breaking into wide smiles.

We hugged and then turned once again toward the door this time hand in hand to head out into the evening where we celebrated both thirty wonderful years of marriage and one small victory over the kind of righteousness that ends all perfectly planned special occasions!

Establishing New Family Commitments. During this stage of marriage, having intentional conversations to clarify your relationship with important family members in your life is critical for you. It is important to reassess your commitments to both your own parents and to your adult children.

Many couples, for instance, find it beneficial to have conversations to clarify their commitments with their adult children and their aging parents in terms of emotional and/or financial support (Mauterstock, 2008). What is your job now that your children are grown and your parents are aging? What are your biggest concerns or fears? What are your biggest hopes for the future? What regrets or resentments do you have toward your aging parents? What worries or concerns do you have with your adult children? How often do you plan to be in communication with your parents and your adult children? How often do you plan to see them? Such conversations can help you to design the kind of relationship you wish to have with your family members in this phase of marriage.

Asking "What's Completing and What's Opening Up?" This fifth stage of marriage is a time when couples assess where they are in life, what is completing in their lives and what new opportunities are opening up for them. If you are at this stage of marriage, you are coming to grips with at what crossroads you now find yourselves. You may feel the ground shifting under your feet, giving way to a new time in your lives that is filled with a mixture of uncertainty and loss with a new sense of freedom and possibility. This is a time to take stock of what you have accomplished and reflect on those dreams you have not yet attained. It is a time when letting go of past disappointments and hurts gives way to a new and exciting time of creativity, fulfillment and contribution.

In 2006, Martha and I wrapped up her expatriate assignment in Amsterdam. Her boss was ready to offer her another position with the company in one of several cities in the United States. Martha and I, however, felt the tug to return to New England, be closer to our eldest daughter and son-in-law who had had their first child in January of that year and to our second daughter who was in college in Boston. I had already shifted my career path rather dramatically four years earlier. After building a career as an administrator in the city of Hartford, as a trainer and educator in corporate executive education and as a pioneer in the field of leadership and change, it was now time for Martha to put her attention on a new career direction.

It was this recognition that we were embarking on a rather significant life transition that was the impetus for Martha to suggest we create that collage and talk about our future. We both wanted to start our own businesses and live in a large, vibrant metropolitan area. I was eager to work with married couples in designing and living extraordinary lives together and Martha was inspired to work in organizations engaged in large-scale change initiatives. Her vision included returning to academia and getting a Ph.D. in the field of leadership and change. Not accepting another position with her company meant that neither one of us would have an income waiting for us back home. We were fully aware that we would have to work together to build our businesses. We had no guarantees. But like when we were first married, we had each other and we saw our future as an exciting adventure.

At this time, Martha and I were entering the fifth phase of partnership marriage. We knew that, standing in partnership, we could create a wonderful new life back home in Boston. We were at a new juncture, however, where it felt we could take nothing for granted. We were at a new crossroads. Two of our three children had grown up and were out of the house. We were transitioning to the "empty nest" stage of life. Grandparenthood was a whole new realm and we were getting used being called Oma and Opa. In addition, we were both surprised at how unprepared we were for re-entry into our own country of origin. I thought coming home to Boston would be like putting on an old, well-worn shirt. I envisioned life in America would be like jumping up on a bicycle and riding it effortlessly after a long hiatus. It wasn't that way. Martha and I had both changed a lot in four years. We weren't just United States citizens anymore. We experienced ourselves as citizens of the larger world.

In the first couple of years back home, we both had a range of feelings, or, maybe more accurately, a rollercoaster of emotions. It was a time of much uncertainty, yet we were grounded in the resourcefulness of our partnership, the power of "us." We leaned into our relationship for support, nurturance and strength. Now more than ever, it was important for us to be focused on the quality of our marriage as we invented our new life in Boston. We talked continuously about the quality of life we wanted to create together.

At this phase of marriage, it is valuable for you to have conversations around what is completing and coming to a close in your lives. Your children may be leaving home and careers may be winding down. What have you accomplished in your lives together? What mountains have you scaled? What challenges have you overcome? What moments of sweet joy have you shared that live for you as if they happened only yesterday? What disappointments or regrets can you let go of or give up? What dreams have you not yet fulfilled? What projects are still left incomplete?

It is also important for you to have conversations around what this new phase of your marriage is like for you and what emotions you are experiencing. What new challenges or obstacles are you facing? What limitations are you now experiencing, physically, financially or otherwise? What are you concerned or fearful about? What is the quality of your life together? What are you thankful for? What do you appreciate about each other and your relationship? What do you celebrate in life now?

And finally, at this stage, you can have conversations around what is opening in your lives. What do you long for? What new dreams are you having? What passions are bubbling up inside? What are you yearning for? What new possibilities do you see? What vision do you now have for your future? What is left to accomplish? What contribution do you want to make to your families, to your community and to the world? What are you up to now?

Dreaming New Dreams. The fifth phase of marriage is not a time to shrink back or to put your feet up and rest. This is the time of your life to start dreaming again and to dream big together. What countries do you want to visit? What adventures to you want to tackle? What book are you thinking of writing? Are you ready to get your Ph.D.? Is it time to start a business individually or together? Is it time to get in shape? How about running a marathon? Where do you want to live? With whom do you want to play? What do you want to contribute?

In this fifth phase, couples in a partnership marriage continue to use their marriage as a platform to fulfill their lives together. They invest in their marriage so they can express what they are passionate about, enjoy their lives and contribute to those around them. It is a time to have conversations "outside the box" and dare to do things you've never done before.

This is not to say this will be easy, without risk or without fear. At this stage, marriage partners see each other's true greatness and don't allow each other to draw back. It is important for you to have conversations in which your considerations, concerns and fears can get expressed and heard. There are many, many tools in this book that you can use to keep moving forward toward your dreams and the future you intend to build!

Creating a New Purpose for Your Marriage. To this point, many couples have had as their main purpose the raising of healthy and happy children and launching them into their own lives. When your children leave home, your contribution as parents takes a different form; your initial purpose as parents begins to change. Your role is less active and your advice and support is usually most welcome when it comes at the request of your adult children. Your primary marital purpose as parents is completing.

Having your children grow up and leave the nest can be disconcerting and stressful for you. Yet, it is also a time in your life that is a wonderful opportunity to create a new purpose for your marriage. This new purpose can be a simple statement of your intentions that are at the heart of the contribution you want to make. This purpose is no longer necessarily just about your own nuclear family. At this stage of life, the purpose of your marriage touches all people who know you.

Zander and Zander (2000) define "vision" as articulating possibility, fulfilling a fundamental desire of humankind, making no reference to morality or ethics and being a freestanding and timeless picture. A co-created vision is your stand for the contribution you are committed to making. You can think of it as creating a purpose. Such a purpose might be "providing visionary, inspired leadership," "living in the presence of wonderment, magic and mystery," or "being self-expressed, magnificent and adventurous."

It often takes time to formulate a purpose for one's life or for one's marriage at this stage. It doesn't happen overnight. Martha and I found ourselves having numerous conversations about the difference we wanted to make at this stage. In our first conversations, we delved into our individual purposes. Each of us had a wealth of experience and wisdom to draw on and we explored our individual contributions. Martha's interest was fostering leadership in purpose-driven companies; mine was helping couples in creating enduring and fulfilling partnership in their marriages. What became clear to us was that we each were interested in being leaders in our own purpose-driven company and we had been committed to being full partners in our marriage. Leadership in life and partnership in marriage, for us, have been two sides of the same coin. You can't have one without the other. Our purpose has changed and morphed as we have worked together. What is exciting is that we are engaged in conversations about our collective purpose together. It has been thrilling to dwell together in the question: What is the difference we want to make at this phase of our lives?

Here are some other questions that you, individually and as a couple, can ask yourselves to discover your unique contribution or purpose. What are you called to do? Where do you want to focus your attention? What is most important to you now? What are your unique gifts as a couple? What can people count on you for? What are you building? What are your intentions? What is the impact you want your marriage to have on others?

For many couples at this time in their lives, purpose for their marriage becomes very simple. Your purpose might be to bring joy into the world. Another purpose might be to love others. Or, your purpose might be to see and acknowledge the greatness in others. The contribution you leave with other people is quite literally the impact others have when they are in your presence. By exploring the contribution you want to make as a couple, you can be intentional about the impact that you have in the world.

Conversations for Clarifying
Your Passion and Contribution

Below, I have given you a couple of conversations you and your spouse can have to help you both clarify what you are passionate about at this stage of your marriage and what contribution you wish to make. By examining at what crossroads you find your lives, you can begin to determine what is important to you both. Re-designing your relationship with your adult children and your aging parents can also help you clarify your role with your family members and carve out that time for your partnership. Visit www.thepartnershipmarriagebook.com/tools and type in the access code "youandme" (no quotes, all lower case) to download The Partnership Marriage Phase Five Toolkit to your computer.

1. Exploring the Crossroads in Your Lives. The challenge of phase five is to begin to acknowledge what is completing in your lives and to notice what is opening up in your lives. It requires you to let go of the past. In this conversation, you have an opportunity to let go of unmet expectations and unrealistic dreams. You can also forgive each other for past hurts and marital disappointments. Converse with each other about what is important to you and what you are passionate about. What excites you? What are you thankful for? What new possibilities for the future do you see?

To set a context for this conversation, imagine that the two of you are dwelling together in a beautiful outdoor place. It can be at the top of a hill or a mountain, on a ship in the middle of the sea, or in a field of flowing wheat. It can be on the Cape or in Texas, anywhere where you feel free and together. It can be in the morning, afternoon or evening. From this place, you want to be able to see in all directions. Take a moment and share together to identify this location where you can get a meta-view of your entire life together; past, present and future. In this place, imagine you are at crossroads in your lives together.

Imagine that you as an individual and you both as partners have lived your entire lives to be here in this present moment. Look back into your past. Your past has brought you to this moment. Your whole life has been on the path to right here, right now. Take a moment and become aware of everything that has happened in the past. Now take a moment and become aware of everything that is going on in your world right now. Finally, take a moment and become aware of everything that will happen in the future. Become aware of all that has happened in your life, is happening and will happen in your life together.

Have a conversation with each other using the following questions. You can use all of them or a few of them. The purpose of these questions is for you to explore at what crossroads you find yourselves at this time in your lives.

- What is in the process of completing in your lives?
- What contribution have you made in your life?
- What do you want to be acknowledged for?
- What disappointments can you let go of?
- What unfulfilled dreams can you let go of?
- For what can you forgive yourself?
- For what can you forgive your partner?
- For what are you thankful?
- What is in the process of opening up in your lives?
- What opportunities are before you?
- What possibilities to do you see?
- What dreams have yet to be fulfilled?
- What are you excited about in your future?

- What contribution do you plan to make?
- What are you grateful for?

You can return to this conversation often to help you to clarify what in your life is completing, what you are present to and what you see your future holds for you.

2. Re-establishing Family Roles. During phase five of partnership marriage, parents are aging, adult children are going to college, starting work, and/or getting married and grandchildren are being born. Having intentional conversations to clarify your commitments to your aging parents and your adult children can be critical for you in dealing successfully and powerfully with these transitions.

Have a conversation using the questions below to evaluate your relationship with your aging parents and your adult children:

- What is your commitment now in your life to your child/parents?
- What do you now see as your job as parents to your adult child/as adult child to your own parents?
- What aspects do you enjoy the most in your relationship with your child/parents?
- What are areas that seem to be the source of the greatest stress in your relationship with your child/parents?
- What do you fear the most in the future concerning you child/parents?
- What regrets do you have in your relationship with your child/parents?
- What resentments do you have in your relationship with your child/parents?

- What are you looking forward to in the future concerning your child/parents?
- What do you want to be acknowledged for in your relationship with your child/parents?
- What do you say is possible now in your relationship with your child/parents?

Such conversations can help the two of you design the kind of relationship you wish to have with your family members.

Chapter

9

WE'RE ENOUGH

CONVERSATIONS FOR COMPLETION, WISDOM AND LEGACY

> *"What greater thing is there for two human souls than to feel that they are joined for life—to strengthen each other in all labor, to rest on each other in all sorrow, to minister to each other in all pain, to be one with each other in silent, unspeakable memories at the moment of the last parting."*
>
> –George Elliot

Phase Six of a Partnership Marriage

This last phase is the completion stage. In this stage, couples have become exemplars of having lived an enduring, fulfilling partnership marriage and are an inspiration to others who seek to have a fulfilling life together. Couples at this stage are sharing activities together, they are still growing and they are finding new ways to play. They know just how short life is. The context of their life is "We're enough" and the sentiment in their marriage is "I deeply appreciate you and our partnership in life."

Older couples have downsized their lives and are spending much more time together at home. They enjoy a whole new time of sharing with each other, caring for each other and enjoying each other's company. It is a time when couples need to re-energize their marriage, find ways to enjoy each other's company, find new meaning in their daily activities and balance "we" time with "me" time (Harrar & DeMaria, 2000).

These couples are coming to grips with what their life together has given them and what realistically won't be fulfilled. They renew their commitment to celebrate what gifts they do have and let go of unfulfilled dreams. They have conversations about what values, traditions and possessions they will leave to their loved ones. They reflect on their life's experiences and on the larger historical context in which their lives played out. They celebrate and honor that. Their conversations focus on being complete, sharing their wisdom and honoring their legacy. The dream they had years in the past of sharing a long and happy life together has been realized and there is much to appreciate.

Partnership may appear to be less active, yet partnership at this stage is a very real part of everyday life. Conversations for taking care of your health, attending to your financial well-being and staying connected with your family and friends are key for you and your spouse at this stage. Physical limitations or financial concerns may limit some kinds of activities, yet you can engage in talking about plans, intentions and dreams, fostering a happy attitude and staying young at heart.

This sixth phase of marriage can be a very special time in your life together. It can be a time of exploration and play. Some couples go on personal journeys to explore their family history through genealogical work together or to write joint reflections of their shared life. Travel may include going to places of historical and ancestral significance or visiting relatives and family members with whom you have lost touch. Participating in local events, such as community plays, musical concerts or new exhibits at the museum in town are great fun and ways to have special dates.

Companionship at this stage of your life is very important. Being together and conversing about your long journey together can nurture you daily. Conversations can be rich with memories of a shared life, reflections of difficult times, recollections of exciting or intimate moments and personal stories of risks taken and of victories won. Write them down. Share them with your friends and family.

At this phase of marriage, there are two central concerns for older couples. How do I (we) maintain control of my (our) life? How do I (we) want to be remembered? It is vitally important that you include your extended family in these conversations (Mauterstock, 2008). Let your family know what is important to you around end of life decisions, financial concerns and what you want to leave to them. Make time to celebrate your partnership, your marriage and your life with your family.

I take inspiration from my parents-in-law, Ruth and Jeff, who in the evening will often have a cocktail or a nightcap before bed and will toast each other, their relationship and their long life together by simply saying, "Enough." It is their expression of deep appreciation for their life partnership and for the gifts their shared life has given them. Every time I hear them say that word, I hear joy, abundance and grace, qualities of their marriage, which will reverberate across generations and bathe our family in love for years to come.

Central Conversations in Phase Six

In phase six of a partnership marriage, there are conversations that you and your spouse can have to explore what is important to you at this stage of life, to share the riches and wisdom of your relationship and to explore what you wish to leave to future generations.

Asking "What's Important to Us Now?" This is a very powerful question that you and your spouse can explore often. This question can help guide what you attend to, what you commit to and what you do. This question can help you to make the decisions and the choices you need to make. This question helps shape how you want to contribute to others and what you want your legacy to be. This very powerful question can help you to determine the quality of your life at this stage of your marriage.

Areas of life that are important to many couples at this phase of life are taking care of their health and well-being, staying in touch with friends and family, nurturing their spiritual life, attending to their financial affairs, and talking about end of life decisions. The following are questions you can explore with each other in each of these life areas: What do we value? What will we focus our attention on? What are we committed to? What concerns do we have? What will we do? Who else can help us to explore these questions? By having these conversations together, with family members and trusted advisors, you can not only identity what's important to you in these areas of life, but you can also take actions that are in alignment with your values and with the lifestyle you wish to create at this time in your marriage.

Reflecting on your Life Together. This sixth stage of marriage is a time of reflection, gratitude and completion. You can take time to have conversations to reflect on your long journey together, your joys and sorrows and your rewards and difficulties, and be cognizant of the richness of your relationship. It can be a time of deep appreciation for a life of shared memories.

There are commitments and opportunities that are coming to completion. Health concerns may be limiting certain kinds of activities, such as travel or getting around independently in the community. You may be dealing with your families' concerns around your driving a car. This is a time when you take stock of what you can do and what you can't do and the risks and challenges involved in the commitments you make.

At this stage of partnership marriage, conversation and sharing together are central to your life. Having conversations for intimate connection and for exploring what you are committed to are just as important now as they were early in your marriage. Engaging in conversations for what is going to support your happiness and well-being remain central in your lives. Continuing to grow, solving problems and being successful together remain essential as well. Having conversations for alignment, balance, passion, fulfillment and contribution remain as crucial now as in the fourth or fifth decade of marriage. Having conversations that nurture your connection, your sense of "us" and your experience of partnership keeps your marriage strong.

In the last stage of your marriage, many of the memories that you converse about not only center on all the things you have done together in your lives, but also all on the important conversations you have had along the way. For instance, you reminisce about what you talked about on your first dates and about when you decided to have children, buy a house or live overseas. You remember the intimate conversations you had sitting on the beach in the Caribbean, nestled in the sleeping bag while camping in the Rockies, or walking along the streets of Paris. You also recall your favorite arguments, for instance, when you argued about how to open a tuna fish can, how to put up wallpaper on the living room wall or how to navigate through the streets of Providence. You share with each other times of conflict and recall the lessons you learned about yourselves, about your relationship and about life itself at those difficult times. You ultimately weave a rich fabric of life together by the conversations you have had over your lifetime.

Sharing the Wisdom and Legacy of Your Partnership Marriage. The wisdom gained in living a fulfilling and enduring marriage becomes one part of the legacy that you give to future generations. An extraordinary opportunity of this phase of partnership marriage is for you to have conversations exploring what your lifetime of commitment has taught you about life and marriage and then to share what you have learned with your family. What are the most important ingredients in a happy and healthy marriage over a lifetime? To what should your loved ones pay attention in order to keep their marriage strong and vibrant? What conversations are most important to forge a lifetime partnership? When problems occur and your marriage feels off track, what recommendations would you give your family? What's most important to know when resolving deep hurts or transgressions in the marriage? What is the purpose of marriage? What makes a marriage truly fulfilling and enduring? When a couple commits to marriage, what, in fact, are they committing to? And lastly, what are the fruits of a lifelong partnership marriage? The lessons you learned as a result of your "lived experience" in a partnership marriage are an exceptional legacy you can leave to future generations.

You can connect to your progeny by sharing what you wish to leave behind and how you wish to be remembered. You may want to be remembered for being loving and generous parents and for having an impact in a community organization (Mauterstock, 2008). You may want to bequeath heirlooms and possessions of significance to family members, write family histories by telling family stories or donating financial gifts to your church or a charitable, non-profit organization. These conversations are important for you to have with your families.

Your long journey as a loving couple helps to shape the lives of your loved ones by affirming that a fulfilling, enduring partnership marriage is, indeed, really possible. You are an exemplar of that commitment in life and an inspiration to your family and future generations.

Conversations for Exploring Your Wisdom and What's Important Now

Below, I have given you a couple of conversations you and your spouse can have to help you both to tap into the wisdom of your marriage and to explore what's important in your lives now. I have additional conversations at www.thepartnershipmarriage.com/tools. You can visit the website and type in the access code "youandme" (no quotes, all lower case) to download The Partnership Marriage Phase Six Toolkit to your computer.

1. Examining What's Important to You at this Stage, Take a few minutes to identify an event or experience that was especially rewarding, special or poignant for you as a couple.

a. Exploring What's Important to You. Consider the following questions:

- What was special, rewarding, poignant and important for your marriage in that experience?
- What was important to you about that experience?

Share two or three central values of your relationship with each other.

b. Expressing Your Values in Life Together. Now begin to speculate as to how you will express the values you just shared with each other in your lives from now on. Looking through the lens of those values, brainstorm all the ways you can express what is important to you.

- What will you attend to?
- What will you be doing?

- What will you be experiencing?
- What will be different from how you are living your lives now?
- What will you be committed to?

c. Living Your Values. Next, converse with each other about what contribution your lives make to the people around you when you are living consistently with your values.

- What contribution are you making (have you made) to your family?
- What contribution are you making (have you made) to your friends?
- What do your marriage and your relationship contribute to others?
- Where in your family and circle of friends do you see your values being expressed?

d. Creating the Collage of Photographs. Next, gather some of your important photographs that express your most important values in your marriage. With glue sticks and a small poster board, create a collage of these photographs. Then, share with each other focusing on these questions:

- What was it like to create your collage together?
- What did you become aware of?
- What did you see about your marriage and the contribution that it has been?
- What do you see about the contribution of your marriage going forward?
- What do you deeply appreciate about your marriage?

2. Exploring the Wisdom of Your Marriage. Have a conversation together about what you would say to your family on how to create and enjoy a fulfilling and enduring partnership marriage over an entire lifetime. Consider the following questions:

- What are the most important ingredients in a happy and healthy marriage over a lifetime?
- What should couples pay attention to in order to keep their marriage strong and vibrant?
- What conversations are most important to forge a lifetime partnership?
- When problems occur and one's marriage feels off track, what recommendations would you give your loved ones?
- What's most important to know when resolving deep hurts or transgressions in the marriage?
- What is the purpose of marriage?
- What makes a marriage truly fulfilling and enduring?
- When a couple commits to marriage, what, in fact, are they committing to?
- What are the fruits of a lifelong partnership marriage?

Chapter

10

A VISION FOR PARTNERSHIP MARRIAGE

"I didn't marry you because you were perfect. I didn't even marry you because I loved you. I married you because you gave me a promise. That promise made up for your faults. And the promise I gave you made up for mine. Two imperfect people got married and it was the promise that made the marriage. And when our children were growing up, it wasn't a house that protected them; and it wasn't our love that protected them—it was that promise."
                                    –Thornton Wilder, *The Skin of Our Teeth*

Martha's and my friendship started with a very simple request and then a promise. "Will you go out on a date with me on Saturday night?" "Yes, I will." A couple of years later, the possibility of our marriage started with an equally simple question and a promise we asked each other. "Will you marry me?" "Yes, I will." Our marriage began the day we promised to take each other as husband and wife. Upon reflection, it is amazing to me that Martha and I dove into life together, as my family likes to point out, so young and with so little preparation. We planned to make it up as we went. We were confident that our marriage was just going to work out. We had our parents, aunts and uncles and grandparents as solid role models. In 1974, getting married seemed to be what everyone was doing right after college.

Today, getting married isn't what everyone does right after college. It is one possible choice, but not the only one. Young adults are often waiting until their late twenties, after they have established their careers, finished graduate school or become financial stable before considering marriage. Marriage is still very important to many young people, but there is greater caution and deliberation before jumping into it. As Cherlin (2009) has written, marriage has now become a capstone or a final accomplishment to becoming an adult. Getting married is something people now choose to do when they are financially and emotionally ready.

There is evidence that the divorce rate has been declining over the last decade. That is good news. The number of people who are choosing marriage, however, is also declining. Recent statistics suggest that, for the first time since marriage statistics have been kept, the percentage of people getting married in the U.S. population has dropped to below 50%. There are many people, particularly high school educated, lower income individuals, who yearn for having a marital partner just as college educated, upper income earners do, but choose to cohabitate rather than get married because they cannot afford to marry. Today, marriage favors those who have an economic advantage.

In the United States today, society is rapidly moving to a time when *all* people, regardless of sexual orientation, will have equal opportunity under the law to get married. Sixty years ago, only heterosexual people could legally marry and, when they did, the main social contract was to have children and raise a family. The purpose of marriage has transformed over the past four decades. When abortion became legal in the 1970s and women were granted the legal right to choose to have children, childbirth became separated from the fundamental design of marriage. Advances in birth control became a significant factor in a woman's choice to have children. Cohabitating couples, single parent families and married couples choosing not to have children have increased. Individuals have focused on finding their life partner with whom they could create a marriage in which they can be self-expressed and fulfilled. Raising children has become one choice, among many, that a couple can make.

Some marriage experts have been concerned that the institution of traditional marriage between a man and a woman has grown more fragile. Their worry exacerbates when they consider extending the legal right to marry to gay and lesbian individuals. The basis for such worry are also statistics showing an increase in the divorce rate since the 1960s, cohabitation as a chosen lifestyle, the number of people in serial marriages and the number of single parent families.

In 2011, a panel of renowned social scientists and marriage experts made thirty specific conclusions around the importance of marriage in American society (Wilcox, 2011). Their report said that children are more likely to thrive, enjoy greater family stability and have better relationships when they grow up in a married family with both their father and their mother. Also, the likelihood of these children failing at marriage later in their own lives decreases. There is also evidence, however, that adolescents who grow up in stable gay and lesbian partnerships do as well as those children who grow up in stable heterosexual families (van Gelderen, et. al., 2012). In fifty years, it will be interesting to study the well-being of children raised in stable homes of legal same-sex marriages of either sex compared to stable heterosexual marriages.

The 2011 panel also found that children of married couples have greater economic advantages because married couples build more wealth than either cohabitating couples or single parents. Children who live in two parent families tend to enjoy better physical health on average, than do children who grow up in other family lifestyles. One wonders what role partnership in long-term marriage will play in fostering happy, healthy children, independent of the genetics, the sex or the sexual orientation of the both parents. My vision is that children will be nurtured, feel loved and grow to their greatest potential in healthy and vibrant families of both heterosexual and same-sex married couples where partnership is a way of relating to each other and a way of living.

At the writing of this book, I have three young grandchildren who will witness the evolution of marriage in the twenty-first century. If they marry when they are grown, they will likely do so in the decade of 2030. If their marriages last at least fifty years, they will be able to reflect on the state of marriage and all that has occurred in the intervening years.

My vision of marriage in the year 2080 is that marriage remains a central organizing institution in American society. All people, regardless of sexual orientation, have the legal right to get married in every state of the union. The choice to have children is still one important choice that a couple can make, but it is not the only choice. Choosing not to have children and pursuing lives oriented around other noble purposes are valued and honored in society. The opportunity for couples in same-sex marriages to raise adopted and/or their own biological children is seen as a normal occurrence, one that is joyful and nurturing for both the children and their parents. There is no stigma or concern that children cannot be cared for just as lovingly in a home of same-sex parents.

I have a vision that the divorce rate has significantly decreased. By 2080, less than 15% of couples who marry get divorced at a later time in their lives. The majority of couples who take their vows together are able to fulfill their dream of a long and happy life together. Not only have couples learned to be responsible for caring for their emotional connection with each other over the long haul, they have also learned how to be true partners in life.

In 2080, the institution of marriage is strong. Marriage works because the couples who choose to marry know that to have an enduring and fulfilling marriage requires constant attention and vigilance. Couples know that they must master many tools and learn to have all kinds of conversations to be successful in life together. Marital education and coaching is readily available for all married couples. Spouses are learning how to listen and how to understand each other. They are learning to clarify what they are committed to and to be aligned in their commitments. Couples are learning how to create a vision of their future and to work together designing projects in partnership to fulfill their individual and joint dreams.

When couples have difficulties in communication or in the fulfillment of their commitments, they have learned effective ways to work together to assess what is happening, to share with each other what's working and not working and to be responsible for taking effective action in partnership. Blaming, defensiveness, being critical and withdrawal are antiquated ways of coping with conflict or problems. Couples early in their relationship learn to recognize the ineffectiveness of operating with each other in such reactive ways when life presents challenges and to shift their assumptions and perspectives so they can be real, effective and creative with each other.

Couples, naturally and with great ease, honor and nurture their relationship. Married couples recognize the quality of their marriage as their top priority. All couples know that research continually demonstrates that couples who put their marriage first live longer, have greater wealth, are happier, are healthier and, even, have better sex lives than couples who don't. Taking care of one's marriage is seen as the single best investment a couple can make. The positive impact of having a marriage that works reverberates across generations. Their children benefit greatly. Children who grow up with happily married parents have role models for learning about what it will take to have a successful partnership *and* marriage.

For individuals who choose other lifestyles, such as not getting married, cohabitating or raising children alone, there is societal acceptance. There is no societal angst about the fragility of marriage. In fact, marriage is seen as strong because the vast majority of marriages are happy, fulfilling and last a lifetime. Regardless of the sexual orientation of marital partners, marriage is a union between two people who view each other as equals and who choose to get married on the basis of unconditional love. In that choice, there is the central recognition that for their marriage to endure, it must work for "you, me *and* us." Being committed to the quality of their relationship means couples routinely communicate and learn to have the conversations necessary to negotiate roles and responsibilities fairly and to work out differences between them to their mutual satisfaction. They are keenly aware that to have their marriage work, they must both be continually expanding their self-awareness and growing emotionally, spiritually and intellectually. They are responsible for their own self-development and committed to that of their partner. By 2080, all couples are aware that while they have a legal right to marry and they don't take that right for granted. It is uniquely their responsibility to have their marriage prosper.

In 2080, I envision that, for a vast majority of couples who choose to marry, being married is a rewarding and joyful state of being. The conversations that are occurring in couples' homes are interesting, stimulating, creative and intimate. Being right and making each other wrong as a way of interacting in marital relationships has all but disappeared. Marriage is viewed as a lifetime partnership. Couples have the conversational tools to create and fulfill their dreams. Commitment, alignment, understanding, play and appreciation have become the fabric of marital life. Finally, the vast majority of couples who marry are living fulfilling lives in which they know that, when they are devoted to their sense of "us" and the quality of their marriage, they share a world where they know anything is possible, they experience each other as full partners and they are wildly passionate about their life's journey together.

BIG SKY

With you, my love, I soar, free, with majesty, the horizon, the future, always within reach, ever bright, ever expanding, always glorious.

Your grace embraces, your beauty stuns, your strength buoys; I am lifted up, carried to the clouds and beyond where the heavens and each moment bind us into one, giving freedom, giving flight.

With you, my beautiful, life is magical, joyful and just plain fun, doubled over in laughter, cheeks aching kind of fun.

With you, wonderment, mystery and "I can't believe my life" are a way of being, a way of living.

With you, life is great, adventurous and "wow," fear goes "poof," I shout "yes" to life.

With you, I am home, at peace. I am bathed in your countenance, the wholeness of your being.

With you, my sweet, I am grounded, like a pillar, a taproot to the center of the earth, two feet planted, ready for life.

With you, my love, I soar, free, with majesty.
You are my big sky.

APPENDIX 1:

PARTNERSHIP UMBRELLA

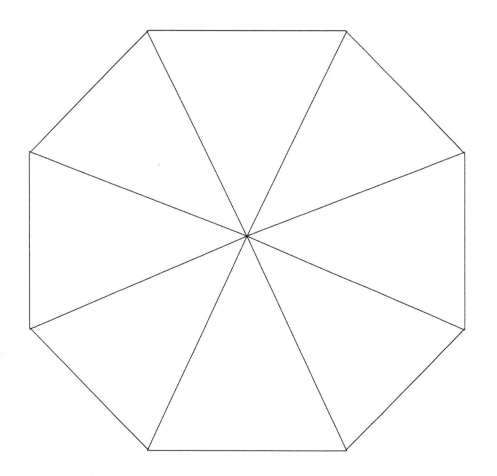

REFERENCES

Arp, D. H., Arp, C. S., Stanley, S. M., Markman, H. J., & Blumberg, S.L. (2001). *Empty Nesting: Reinventing your marriage when the kids leave home.* San Francisco, California: Jossey-Bass.

Baltes P. B. (1997). On the incomplete architecture of human ontogeny: Selection, optimization, and compensation as foundation of developmental theory. *American Psychologist,* 52, 366-80.

Baltes, P. B., Staudinger, U.M., and Lindenberger, U. (1999). Life span psychology: Theory and application to intellectual functioning. *Annual Review of Psychology,* 50, 471-507.

Bohm, D. (1996). *On Dialogue.* New York, New York: Routledge.

Cherlin, A.J. (2009). *The Marriage-Go-Round: The state of marriage and family in America today.* New York, New York: Alfred A. Knopf.

Cohn, D., Passel, J., Wang, W., & Livingston, G. (2011). *Barely half of U.S. adults are married – A record low.* Washington, D.C.: Pew Research Center.

Collins, G. (2009). *When everything changed.* New York, New York: Little, Brown and Company.

Coontz, S. (2005). *Marriage, a history: How love conquered marriage.* New York, New York: Penguin Books.

Czeslaw, M. (1983). *Visions of San Francisco Bay.* New York, New York: Farrar Straus Giroux.

Doherty, W. J. (2001). *Take back your marriage: Sticking together in a world that pulls us apart.* New York, New York: The Guilford Press.

Fowers, B. (2000). *Beyond the myth of marital happiness: How embracing the virtues of loyalty, generosity, justice and courage can strengthen your relationship*. San Francisco, California: Jossey-Bass, Inc. Publishers.

Geiseman, O.A. (1946). *Make yours a happy marriage*. Saint Louis, Missouri: Concordia Publishing House.

Gilbert, L. A. & Rachlin, V. (1987). Mental health and psychological functioning of dual-career families. *The Counseling Psychologist*, 15, 7–49.

Gottman, J. M. (1994). *Why marriages succeed or fail: And how you can make yours last*. New York, New York: Simon and Schuster.

Harrar, S. & DeMaria, R. (2007). *The seven stages of marriage: Laughter, intimacy, and passion, today, tomorrow, and forever*. Pleasantville, New York: Reader's Digest.

Lawrence-Lightfoot, S. (2009). *The third chapter: Passion, risk, and adventure in the 25 years after 50*. New York, New York: Sarah Crichton Books.

Mauterstock, R. (2008). *Can we talk: A financial guide for baby boomers assisting their elderly parents*. Rogers, Arizona: Soaring with Eagles Publisher.

Miser, A. & Miser, M. (2009). Couples coaching for expatriate couples: A sound investment for international businesses. In Moral, M.C. and Abbott, G. (2009), *The Routledge Companion to International Business Coaching*. New York, New York: Routledge.

Miser, A. & Rosano, S. (2006). From challenge to joy: Transforming common dilemmas for parents raising children with developmental and medical disabilities. Unpublished manuscript.

Miser, M. (2006). *Vision: The engine of change*. Unpublished maunscript.

Nichols, M.P. (1994) *The lost art of listening: How learning to listen can improve relationships*. New York, New York: The Guilford Press.

Patterson, J.M. (1991). Family resilience to the challenge of a child's disability. *Pediatric Annals*, 20(9), 491-499.

Rosenberg, M. (2005). *Non-violent communication: A language of life*. Encinitas, California: Puddle Dance Press

Smith, C.E. (1994). The Merlin factor: Leadership and strategic intent. *Business Strategy Review*, 5(1), 67.

Stanley, S.M. (2005). *The power of commitment: A guide to lifelong love.* San Francisco, California: Josey-Bass.

Stanley, S.M. & Markman, H.J. (1992). Assessing commitment in personal relationships. *Journal of Marriage and the Family*, 54, 595-608.

Steil, J. M. (1997). *Marital equality: Its relationship to the well-being of husbands and wives.* London, England: Sage Publications.

Twist, L. (2003). *The soul of money: Reclaiming the wealth of our inner resources.* New York, New York: W.W. Norton & Company, Inc.

van Gelderen, L., Bos H., Gartrell N., van Rooij, F.B., Hermanns, J. & Perrin, E. (2012). Quality of life of adolescents raised from birth by lesbian mothers. *Journal of Developmental & Behavioral Pediatrics.* 33(1), 1-7.

Waite, L. J. & Gallagher, M. (2000). *The case for marriage.* New York, New York: Broadway Books.

Weiner-Davis, M. (2001). *The divorce remedy: The proven 7-step program for saving your marriage.* New York, New York: Fireside

Whitworth, L., Kimsey-House, H, & Sandahl, P. (1998). *Co-active coaching: New skills for coaching people towards success in work and in life.* Palo Alto, California: Davies-Black Publishing.

Wilcox, W.B. (2011). *Why marriage matters, third edition: Thirty conclusions from the social sciences.* New York, New York: The Institute for American Values.

Zander, B., & Zander, R. S. (2000). *The art of possibility: Transforming professional and personal life.* Boston, Massachusetts: Harvard Business School Press.

Made in the USA
Charleston, SC
08 July 2014